CHURCH AND STATE IN SOCIAL WELFARE

CHURCH AND STATE

IN SOCIAL WELFARE

BERNARD J. COUGHLIN

COLUMBIA UNIVERSITY PRESS

New York and London 1965

Bernard J. Coughlin, s.j., is the Dean of the School
of Social Service at Saint Louis University.

To
Gene and Celeste
Pat, Larry, Donald
and
Marilyn

FOREWORD

THE PAST decade has witnessed significant and widespread discussion of the role of church and state—discussion which has given little attention to that aspect of the problem relating to social welfare programs. This neglect is indeed surprising in view of the importance and size of both governmental and sectarian social welfare organizations and their increasing number of relationships.

In spite of the growth of large public welfare programs, which make the designation "social welfare state" realistic in terms of the trends in the United States, the voluntary agency occupies an important role in the American community.

The large number of voluntary social welfare agencies in the United States continues to amaze interested foreign visitors. Several thousand voluntary hospitals, several hundred national voluntary organizations, some of which have tens of thousands of local chapters and units, homes for the aged and for children, family agencies, settlement houses, community centers, and numerous other organizations constitute a gigantic effort to assist in the amelioration and prevention of numerous social problems through voluntary efforts.

This American penchant for voluntary effort in social welfare has continued to grow since Alexis de Tocqueville first commented upon the proliferation of American voluntary organizations in the 1830s. The past thirty-five years, however, have seen another fantastic growth—that of governmental programs in the social welfare field. In 1964, the cost of public income maintenance programs alone —social insurance, public assistance, various veterans' and government pensions, and miscellaneous payments—was more than 36 billion dollars.

It was inevitable that the growth of these government welfare programs would raise many questions and critical issues centering on the relationships of these gigantic public services and the long-established social welfare activities under voluntary auspices. The dominant philosophy in the Federal government programs of the 1930s emphasized the necessity of maintaining a sharp differentiation between government and voluntary welfare programs. This policy gradually changed as hospitals, homes for the aged, and other social agencies began to receive Federal, state, and local government funds either as subventions or through some type of purchase of services. Today, hundreds of millions of dollars are spent by government agencies to support voluntary welfare programs or to pay voluntary agencies for services rendered in research, child care, medical services, homes for the aged, and numerous other related activities.

Nor are the complicated and complex relationships of governmental and voluntary effort confined to financial considerations. Government has been exercising increasing control and supervision over voluntary welfare programs through legal requirements in incorporation, licensing of agencies, insistence on standards before payment for services, and various legal and administrative regulations binding upon voluntary organizations.

As a result, many important questions have been the subject of discussion about these government-voluntary relationships. Are voluntary agencies surrendering their independence in accepting government funds? In what areas should government purchase the services of voluntary agencies? Can an operating partnership be developed that will utilize the best programs and efforts of each? Is it desirable to have such a partnership? These are only a few of the scores of questions which are currently debated in social welfare circles, but they indicate the type of discussion being carried on.

It is to be expected that these many questions and issues should concern the sectarian-sponsored welfare agencies. The thousands of social agencies under sectarian auspices—Protestant, Catholic, Jewish —have a vital interest in the direction that relationships between voluntary and government welfare agencies will take. With some sectarian agencies receiving a major portion of their total expenditures from government sources, with others adjusting their programs to meet the demands of government agencies, and with others changing their programs entirely because of government activities, Father Coughlin's comment must be readily accepted: "One of the most important decisions that social welfare must make concerns the position of voluntary welfare in a social-welfare state."

In spite of the importance of the problem, there has been little comprehensive examination of it. As Father Coughlin's study indicates, even those agencies which receive government funds have no clear policy with reference to their government relationships. Nor have they given much attention to the perennial question that arises whenever church-related activities touch government, namely, the church-state question.

Father Coughlin's study and conclusions raise many controversial issues. Many persons may disagree with some of his comments and conclusions, but he has tackled the subject frankly and posed the basic problems and questions clearly. His analysis of sectarian agency–government relationships is, I believe, the most comprehensive presentation of this subject to appear in the last decade. Of particular significance is his analysis of the philosophies of Protestant, Catholic, and Jewish groups and his conclusion that these three religious groups have different conceptions of their role in society and in social welfare. These differences make any consistent philosophy between government and church- or sectarian-sponsored welfare agencies extremely difficult. Father Coughlin's plea for cooperation among the church groups in facing the issues involved comes at a time when government programs are expanding and church-related welfare organizations appear to be developing greater interest in these expanding programs and in exploring cooperative arrangements with government agencies.

Whatever may be the ultimate direction of church-government relations in social welfare, Father Coughlin's book will make a contribution in bringing needed factual data to bear upon current discussions.

Charles I. Schottland

Brandeis University

PREFACE

THIS is a study of the role of voluntary welfare in our nation's total welfare program. The direction of the study has shifted several times before coming to the form presented here. At whatever stage of the development of my thought and presentation of this manuscript I have been greatly encouraged and assisted by many colleagues.

Charles I. Schottland first interested me in the subject of the study and the many issues that it involves.

To David G. French is due the recognition of hours of fruitful discussion about the definition of the problem and its social policy implications and to Arthur J. Vidich recognition of assistance especially in structuring the presentation of the study.

One group of nationally recognized social welfare executives and professors cooperated in the study in a significant way: discussion with them helped me to experience and appreciate the role of voluntary welfare in our society, and because of their assistance it was possible to extend the scope of the study to the local agencies of their denominations. These executives are Msgr. Raymond J. Gallagher, Secretary, National Conference of Catholic Charities; the Rev. Osgoode H. McDonald, Secretary, Division of Institutional Ministries, American Baptist Home Mission Society; Robert Morris, Professor of Social Planning, Brandeis University; the Rev. Kenneth E. Nelson, Executive Secretary, Division of Health and Welfare Services, The National Council, Protestant Episcopal Church; Olin

E. Oeschger, General Secretary, Board of Hospitals and Homes of the Methodist Church; the Rev. Lee W. Rockwell, Executive Secretary, the Commission on Health and Welfare Services, Evangelical and Reformed Church (United Church of Christ); Charles I. Schottland, Dean and Professor of Social Welfare, Brandeis University; Foy Valentine, Executive Secretary, the Christian Life Commission of the Southern Baptist Convention; the Rev. William J. Villaume, formerly Executive Director, Department of Social Welfare, National Council of the Churches of Christ in the U.S.A.; the Rev. Henry J. Whiting, Executive Secretary, Division of Welfare, National Lutheran Council.

Finally, acknowledgment is due to June Kirkpatrick for assistance in statistical computations, to Frances Bittner and Beth Rogers for editing, and to Ruth Southern and Sharon Allen for typing the manuscript. Special recognition is due to Gloria Ambrosini for her secretarial and research assistance.

To the many others both in government and voluntary welfare whom I interviewed and to the directors of the health and welfare agencies who participated in the study, I wish to express my thanks and appreciation.

One personal word—I have tried to view all sides of an issue in their most favorable light and to consider and present all issues mindful of their delicacy and of the sensitivities of the people whom they affect. If I have not always succeeded, I beg the understanding of the reader.

Bernard J. Coughlin, s.j.

Saint Louis University
July, 1964

CONTENTS

CHURCH AND STATE IN SOCIAL WELFARE

1

TWO WELFARE PHILOSOPHIES

ONE of the most important decisions that social welfare must make concerns the position of voluntary welfare in a social welfare state. The expanding size and increasing number of government welfare programs would seem to call for an overall welfare policy.[1] Such a policy issue may be stated as a question: What is the role of voluntary social welfare in the social welfare state?[2] Stemming from this issue is a second, more delicate question: What is the role of church-related welfare programs in the welfare state? Both issues involve not only history and political philosophies but the relationship of church and state and the various and complex emotions engendered by this relationship.

[1] The terminology *government welfare* will be used to designate those welfare programs and services undertaken by statutory mandate of city, state, and Federal governments and financed through tax funds. *Voluntary welfare* will designate programs and services undertaken and administered independently of statutory mandate and financed in whole or in part philanthropically. The traditional terms *public* (government) and *private* (voluntary) originally used to designate primarily the clientele have become increasingly less serviceable because the lines between a public and a private clientele have become increasingly blurred. The terms *government* and *voluntary* seem more apt because they designate more accurately the motivating sources, the administrative authorities, and the locus of financial responsibilities of the two welfare programs.

[2] No political overtones are intended by the term *welfare state*. In this study *welfare state* is a descriptive term used to designate the present-day democratic state that has actually assumed more comprehensive social responsibility and authority in order to meet what seem to be the demands of an expanding industrialized society.

The role of voluntary welfare in the modern welfare state is determined by either of two divergent social philosophies. For the sake of clarifying policy positions and issues, these two social philosophies will be presented in this chapter as two pure types. The use of typologies is an accepted analytical device for sharply presenting contrasting social theories and the corollary propositions associated with them. The pure types of social philosophies presented here are rarely represented in such a stark manner in actual life, but are polar positions on a continuum that reaches from an absolute welfare-state point of view to complete laissez-faire. Particular welfare groups—government and voluntary, sectarian and nonsectarian—locate themselves somewhere along this continuum in the answer they give to the question: What is the role of voluntary welfare in the modern state?

The first pure type assigns primary responsibility to government welfare. Voluntary welfare is proper to a laissez-faire social structure; in a society dominated by the principle of state welfarism, those functions formerly performed by voluntary associations are functions appropriate to the new legislative welfare program. Voluntary social welfare is therefore a natural component of the laissez-faire state; in the modern welfare state, however, social need should be met by full-scale government programs. Until such time as this is feasible, voluntary welfare effort should continue where need demands, but ultimately its role will diminish to zero. In the interim it should continue to experiment, pioneer, and discover social need; but when and where these functions can be performed by government welfare, voluntary agencies should relinquish them to government.

Several propositions follow from this pure type. First, tax-financed legislated services should develop and function independent of voluntary services. The only significant contact between the two is at that point where voluntary agencies, having ascertained needs or formulated improved methods, urge the creation of government welfare programs. Once programs have been established through legislation, voluntary agencies then move on to other fields, retaining with reference to their former services only a critical eye for the government programs. Voluntary agencies must know when to "move out," and government agencies must know when to "move in," as voluntary programs seek to work themselves out of one job and into another.

Second, there should exist no policy of subsidy to voluntary programs nor any continuous, permanently established program for purchase of the services of voluntary agencies.[3] Both practices tend to impede the development of government services and to put off the day when the government agency would move in to a field of function that is its recognized responsibility. Both types of assistance to voluntary programs—subsidy and purchase of services—are nothing more than political rationalizations by which government avoids its responsibility in welfare. At best, such tax aid to voluntary welfare is a halfhearted way of fulfilling this responsibility and thus perpetuates voluntary services beyond their usefulness as agencies of experimentation and demonstration.

Third, the development and interrelationship of government and voluntary welfare should follow the same pattern as that of public and private education. As the private schools were the forerunners of public education, voluntary welfare is a forerunner of a system of total government welfare. Private schools entered the field first; when they were unable to meet the growing need for education, the governmental school system was conceived. According to the typology, the development of public welfare services will repeat the history of the development of public education.

The second pure typology of the role of voluntary welfare in the modern welfare state assigns primary responsibility to voluntary welfare. Ideally all welfare functions should be carried on by the family or by voluntary welfare associations that grow out of the family or neighborhood. In this way responsibility is kept close to the family unit. Even in a welfare state, voluntary welfare should be a permanent part of the social structure and should carry, beyond experimentation and demonstration, a full-scale service program in the total welfare effort. Even though the modern state

---

[3] *Subsidy* is a lump sum grant by a government agency to a voluntary agency. *Purchase of service* is a per capita payment by a government agency to a voluntary agency in lieu of the services provided by the voluntary association to those persons for whom government recognizes responsibility.

must assume many responsibilities that were either unnecessary or unrecognized in a purely laissez-faire society, there should be a place for a permanent, durable voluntary welfare structure. Moreover, functions that are presently performed by government welfare should be relinquished to voluntary effort when conditions arise and when a pattern of planning makes this possible.

Several propositions follow from this pure type. First, a more sustained and permanent form of planning and cooperation between governmental and voluntary agencies is necessary. Although the state has responsibility for meeting welfare needs, the instrument that the state uses need not be governmental. Rather, responsibility should be carried, if possible, by local functional groups and associations working in cooperation with government. And only in default of voluntary welfare should government welfare become directly responsible. Government therefore should know when to move out and should assist voluntary welfare to move in to meet welfare needs.

Second, since financial aid is an important factor in maintaining the vitality of individual responsibility, cooperation between government and voluntary agencies should in many cases take the form of governmental financial assistance to voluntary welfare. This assistance may take various forms—capital construction, subsidy, purchase of service—whereby government uses voluntary agencies and initiative rather than establish agencies and offer services of its own.

Implied in the first two consequences is a third, that the pattern of welfare should not follow that of education. Whatever may be the merits of the policy followed in education, the need to maintain prior responsibility for welfare with voluntary associations implies that government assist financially and help strengthen voluntary sectarian and nonsectarian associations rather than establish a government welfare structure that functions independently of the voluntary structure.

These typologies relevant to the role of voluntary welfare in modern society and to the relationship of government and voluntary welfare are directed to public policy issues of significant proportions. The role of voluntary welfare and its relationship to government must ultimately be based on a philosophy of social structure.

Ideological questions arise that must be answered practically. How should the welfare state through its agencies be related to voluntary services? Should the state ignore them and compete with them? Or should it use them by cooperating with them? How should the voluntary agencies be related to the welfare state? Should they mistrust the leviathan and strengthen their own house? Or should they cooperate with government and risk the loss of their identity and their long tradition of service? [4]

The social philosophy on which we base the answers to these pressing policy questions will determine the development and pattern of our social welfare structure. This study aims at exploring certain policies and practices in social welfare in order to arrive at a sound policy base from which to answer the question: What is the role of voluntary welfare in the modern welfare state?

[4] The effect that government welfare policies have on voluntary programs is frequently referred to; and while this study is not primarily directed to this area, many of the considerations of the study are tangential to it. There is another side to the coin, however, that is frequently overlooked, the effect that voluntary welfare policies have on government programs. Perhaps some of the considerations in this present study will stimulate a student of social policy to investigate the mutual influence of government and voluntary welfare.

2

THREE THEMES

THROUGHOUT the discussions, workshops, and seminars that are addressed to the problem we have outlined three themes recur like threads in a tapestry. They are three characteristics of modern society, three related problems or variables, that are relevant to the discussion of the role of voluntary welfare in a welfare society. These themes have different meaning to the parties that are involved in determining this role and vary in importance to those who discuss them and are concerned about them. They are particularly significant to us here because current policies and practices pertaining to the central problem of this study—the role of voluntary welfare in the welfare state—are made with an eye to these three themes. Therefore, it is necessary to hear them and to understand their relevance to the question of our study. They will be familiar themes to some readers, but they bear repeated hearing and analysis. They will be stated here only briefly and in their boldest outlines; their full meaning and relevance to this total study will become clearer as the study unfolds.

THE DYNAMICS OF POWER

First there is the theme of the dynamics of political power in a democratic society. Charismatic power,[1] as Weber understands it, is transitory because it is based on the personal strength of a leader to win a following. In a more rationally structured society, power tends to become institutionalized. In the transition from a laissez-

[1] See Gerth and Mills, eds., *From Max Weber*, pp. 245–52.

faire to a structured society, personal qualities are gradually absorbed by institutional roles and functions and ultimately become identical with them. Throughout this metamorphosis from power as personal to power as a role and a function performed by a person, control by men fades and control by institutions dawns.

The sociological effects of the change from charismatic power to power as a role and a function of a social institution are highly significant. First, the power process no longer consists primarily of the influence of individual on individual. Second, power is identified with the social role into which society casts the individual and becomes stabilized in that role. Third, the objective of power is social control for the achievement of the collective aim of the institution.[2]

The institutionalization of power introduces the principle of delegation of power. As society grows, the increasing need for organization carries with it the need for separate levels of administration for the carrying out of specific objectives. Administrative government in turn demands trained leaders. These leaders come to constitute a professional class, which is ultimately regarded as having an official status. By their training and their function in government, they are set apart as a class of political experts, an administrative and organizational elite with a *de jure*, if not also a *de facto*, power to command. In Michels' dictum, the mere fact of "organization implies the tendency to oligarchy." [3] By its nature every organization has aristocratic tendencies, for as an organization grows, roles and functions on all levels of authority—superior and subordinate—divide and subdivide until "there is . . . constituted a rigorously defined and hierarchical bureaucracy." [4]

In a democracy certain dynamic tendencies set a democracy against itself.[5] Thus, Mannheim says that democracies are destroyed not from without by nondemocratic enemies but from within: "They collapse as a result of the working of the innumerable self-neutralizing factors that develop within the democratic system." [6]

---

[2] Mannheim, *Freedom, Power and Democratic Planning*, p. 52.
[3] Michels, *Political Parties*, p. 33.   [4] *Ibid.*, p. 34.
[5] Gerth and Mills, *From Max Weber*, p. 226.
[6] Mannheim, *Sociology of Culture*, p. 174.

There are also socio-psychological effects of the institutionalization of power. Democracies foster freedom and autonomy of the
individual, but to individuals not sufficiently mature to bear the
responsibility that accompanies freedom, freedom is a burden.
Where it is a burden, there are incentives to give it up and "to fuse
one's self with somebody or something outside of one's self in order
to acquire the strength which the individual self is lacking." [7] Thus,
democracies develop mechanisms that induce individuals to surrender their autonomy: "Democracy officially emancipates the individual; actually, however, the latter tends to abdicate the right
to follow his own conscience to seek refuge in the anonymity of
the mass." [8]

This surrender involves a double socio-psychological mechanism.
The masses of the people, pressured by feelings of inferiority, seek
out a superior social power upon whom to rely. Their feeling of
inferiority is satisfied by their dependence on other people or on
an institutional power. They find security in the institutional framework and find a new pride in participating in its power. Their own
self-identity and the meaning of life are determined by this institutional power into which they have submerged, the institution
being at various eras in history sometimes the state, sometimes the
church, sometimes the race, and sometimes the classless society.[9]

At the same time the elite in society, the professional leaders and
the officials, are also pressured by a need to control and by tendencies to make others dependent on themselves or on the institutionalized power with which they identify. This need is unconscious
and is rationalized into a necessity: "I rule over you because I know
what is best for you, and in your own interests you should follow
me without opposition." [10]

The insecure individuals in what Fromm calls a "masochistic"
society seek security in an institutional framework. The cost of
this security is high:

[7] Fromm, *Escape from Freedom*, p. 141.
[8] Mannheim, *Sociology of Culture*, p. 174.
[9] Fromm, *Escape from Freedom*, p. 156.
[10] *Ibid.*, p. 144.

One surrenders one's own self and renounces all strength and pride connected with it, one losses one's integrity as an individual and surrenders freedom; but one gains a new security and a new pride in the participation in the power in which one submerges. One gains also security against the torture of doubt.[11]

But if the price is high, there is return value—freedom from the necessity to make decisions, freedom from responsibility for oneself, freedom from the responsibility to understand the meaning of life. These questions are answered by the individual's relationship to the power by which he has been absorbed: "The meaning of his life and the identity of himself are determined by the great whole into which the self has submerged." [12]

FREEDOM AND RESPONSIBILITY

The counterpart to the theme of power is the theme of personal freedom and responsibility. The dynamism whereby institutional power tends to increase and the individual tends to relinquish personal responsibility by seeking identification with the large society raises questions not only of a threat to freedom but especially of the responsibility of the individual for himself and for the social structure.

In modern society, freedom, like power, is more than an attribute of the individual. Both are institutional realities. If power no longer has meaning apart from institutions, neither has freedom any guarantee or fulfillment apart from them. In the large society men depend upon and identify with institutions that give them security; they likewise depend upon institutions to protect and guarantee their freedom. "In an age of mass organization," says Mannheim, "it is not enough to guarantee rights to individuals, it is equally important to protect the liberties of groups and associations." [13]

Freedom implies responsibility, and the guarantee of freedom is not for the sake of freedom alone but for the sake of keeping the individual responsible for the social order. It was on the basis of personal responsibility that Pius XII distinguished between "the

11 *Ibid.*, p. 156.   12 *Ibid.*
13 Mannheim, *Freedom, Power and Democratic Planning*, p. 280.

people" and "the masses." "The people," he said, "lives and moves by its own life energy; the masses are inert of themselves and can only be moved from outside." [14] The strength or the weakness of a society depends on the spirit by which that society lives. A strong society is a society dominated by the people: "The people lives by the fulness of life and the men that compose it, each of whom—in his proper place and in his own way—is a person conscious of his own responsibility and of his own views." [15] A weak society is a society dominated by the masses: "The masses . . . waiting for the impulse from the outside, becomes an easy plaything in the hands of anyone who seeks to exploit their instincts and impressions." [16]

Thus, the presence or absence of a personal freedom that is socially responsible distinguishes strong from weak societies. In a strong society the human tendency to regress to the irresponsibility of the masses is checked when the citizenry, conscious of its right to self-determination, assumes social responsibility. Regressive tendencies in some social areas and the means to check them are familiar. In the family, for example, the psychodynamic process of maturation is well-known—a process that begins with a close and protective relationship of parent and child and terminates in a healthy security and independence. Through responsible activity and achievement the child develops a sense of his own identity and ultimately comes to have a sense of self-esteem and personal responsibility. Parents who overprotect a child because of their own need to feel wanted or because they themselves have no sense of their own identity endanger the maturity and responsible freedom of the child. The result is neither a healthy child nor a healthy family.

Ultimately, the difference between a strong and a weak society is the difference between the people and the masses. A weak society is resourceless and immobile because it can rely on only a few social groups; a strong society is self-moving and self-determining because it has within itself functional groups each with a life and activity of its own. In a weak society there are few integrated, organic groups which absorb the energies of individuals and offer the

[14] Pius XII, *Christmas Message, 1944*, par. 23.
[15] *Ibid.*   [16] *Ibid.*, par. 24.

means of social fulfillment that stabilize the human person in a community.

A healthy democracy seeks ways to combine the power that large society wields with a citizenry that is free and socially responsible. Mannheim sees one significant element in a balanced democracy, those primary and secondary "organic groups" which he conceives as "useful counterweights" for the sadistic mechanisms that goad mass regression toward social irresponsibility.[17] Because these groups provide the ground for the social roots of the human being, they nurture in him stability and a sense of belonging to the larger society. By absorbing human energies and frustrations, they fill a basic human need—identification with functionally diverse activities and satisfaction from them. The voluntary small associations "canalize and direct" toward the particular ends of the groups [18] the energies and frustrations that, unabsorbed, would initiate regression into mass tendencies. Voluntary associations thus resist social regression and immersion into the great whole.

RELIGION AND SOCIAL CONTROL

Thirdly, there is the theme played by religion and the social control it exercises in society. Social control is written into the very nature of religion. The etymology of the word "religion" is *religare*—to bind together. The primary meaning of the word is theological—to bind men to God. The word also has a sociological meaning—to bind men together in society. It is the second definition that interests sociologists and brings religion within the scope of their thinking. When the sociologist speaks of religion, he is referring not to a particular creed or denomination but to a social institution which aims at exercising a unifying influence on the members of society.

From a theological point of view, religion is grounded in the soul of the human being and makes a total claim to his allegiance. Thus, it has been historically the most profoundly influential insti-

---

[17] Mannheim, *Freedom, Power and Democratic Planning*, p. 92.
[18] Mannheim, *Man and Society*, p. 62.

tution of social control. Other institutions effect a social unity maintained by a pattern of secular custom, convention, and law. Religion effects a social unity of will and a common dedication that is based on conscience. Because man desires a social unity more fundamental than that maintained by custom and law, society attempts to provide the more intensive, internalized social control necessary to satisfy this desire. The source of this control is religion. So fundamental to society is this internal form of social control that once the religion of society is shattered, the social organization continues for a while to work as usual. When a major crisis occurs, however, the walls of society begin to break, for mutual obligations are valid only if they are rooted in conscience, and conscience receives its validity from the religious relationship of men to God and to one another in God.[19]

Precisely, however, because religion is by its nature a thoroughly integrative force, it can be thoroughly divisive, disruptive, and even destructive.[20] Under such conditions religion is socially dysfunctional. From many aspects the history of religion in America is one of increasing social dysfunction. Formerly one religion predominated and was an integrative force in society, but with the rise of Catholicism and Judaism and the fissioning of Protestantism, religion in America became pluralistic, began to lose its unifying power, and became a socially disruptive force.

Two things happen when religion loses its social control function. First, when it becomes socially dysfunctional, it separates man from man and tends to become also theologically dysfunctional, separating man from God. One dysfunctional element breeds the other. Second, when religion fails in its function of fundamental, integrative social control, some other institution—usually the state—attempts to substitute for religion and achieve that social control whose exercise belongs to the very nature of religion.

It is this second effect that is of concern here. When one institution does not fulfill its obligation of social control, others must supply it; when religion is no longer the source of social control based on conscience, some other institution must substitute. In

[19] Mannheim, *Freedom, Power and Democratic Planning*, pp. 19–20.
[20] Nottingham, *Religion and Society*, p. 16.

American society many important functions of religion have been taken over by the state and by the economic order.[21] Thus, it has happened that in today's society the primary sanction for social obligations comes from external patterns of custom, convention, and law—from political, economic, and social institutions.

But there is a further step in the removal of internalized social control from the hands of religion. When the family, labor and industrial organizations, and cultural groups fail to fulfill their social control functions, the state must see to it that these functions are fulfilled through some other means. When religion fails to guarantee to society the necessary social control that is based on conscience, the state, whose proper function is control by secular custom and law, assumes the role proper to religion. At this point, says Nottingham, the question "How secular can one get?" has not only religious relevance but sociological significance: "Can the secular institutions do the minimum integrative job essential for society without borrowing back, as it were, some of the reinforcement of the sacred values previously abandoned?" [22]

When religious integration and control based on conscience no longer exist in society, then the state must borrow back religious values and functions. To carry off this new role, the state must reinvest itself with the aura of the sacred and claim the total allegiance of the members of society, not on secular grounds of efficient service but on the quasi-religious grounds that the state or the society is an end in itself.[23] Such a social condition is secularism.

The growing presence of a secular social climate is of concern to the churches, since it is a climate of indifference to religion, which is seen as hostility to religious values. Confronted with this climate the church senses that it is losing its hold on society and usually reacts in one of two ways. Rather than confront society with its own religious values, the church either accommodates itself to society and reflects society's values or withdraws from society in order to safeguard the purity of its own values. Neither policy has been very effective either in recapturing from secular institutions the social control function that the church believed to be

[21] *Ibid.,* p. 24.   [22] *Ibid.*   [23] *Ibid.*

proper to religion or in rediscovering an internalized principle of social control that is based on conscience.

The relevance to our question of these three themes will become increasingly clear especially as we study the role of the churches in social welfare as that role is determined by the image the churches have of themselves as social institutions and by the social role that society assigns to the churches as reflected in the law.

3

THE SOCIAL ROLE OF
THE CHURCHES

THE self-image the church has of its social role is an important determinant of the policies the church pursues. This image generally stems from certain theological premises and social philosophy orientations, as well as certain factors of social history. The purpose of this chapter is to examine the different role conceptions of the three religious groups.

PROTESTANTISM

Every religion faces a dilemma: it must organize itself to withstand worldliness and perpetuate its message, and it must nourish in the individual those mystical qualities he needs to find God. Mystical qualities elude organization. At least sociologically speaking, "the thoroughgoing mystic is potentially an anarchist as far as organization is concerned." [1] For Catholicism the dilemma is not so marked as it is for Protestantism. Catholicism fosters mysticism within the organizational structure of the church, which it considers a means toward mystical union with God; Protestantism tends to regard institutional organization as not amenable to mysticism.

Neither Lutheranism nor Calvinism—and they contain more institutional elements than most Protestant denominations—has resolved

[1] Nottingham, *Religion and Society*, p. 59n.

the dilemma, which Troeltsch expressed as "the reconciliation of the free inwardness, regulated by conscience, of individual religious conviction with the requirements of a Society based on a common cultus and administration." [2]

Organizational Structure

The dilemma arises out of Reformation theology, which excluded a sacramental system for the communication of grace at the hands of ecclesiastical, sacerdotal authority.[3] This exclusion followed from the exclusion of organized authority and shifted the religious center of gravity from salvation and justification to "personal subjective conviction" and "the emotional experience of a sense of sin and of peace of heart." [4] In this way Protestantism opened the door to the spiritualists and invited in an individualism that not only had no need for organizational structure but also opposed it. Thus, Protestant theology, for which individualism was both breeding ground and nourishment, was at home in laissez-faire American society.[5] In a world of organized bureaucracy, however, it is less at home, the new social structure being less fitted to the spirit of Protestantism, which feels handicapped in the struggle of large power institutions.[6] Because Protestantism is "a weaker religion from the point of view of church organization," [7] it confronts the modern world of ideas with "less resisting power than Catholicism." [8]

There are, of course, differences in the institutional strength of the various Protestant denominations. The episcopal type of church approximates the hierarchical structure of the Catholic church. The presbyterian type is oligarchic, the authority of the ministers being subject to a group of top-ranking colleagues. The congregational type places maximum authority in the individual, each congregation being empowered to choose and counsel its minister and to conduct the administrative affairs of the church. The congregational type of church, in which the minister has no more

---

[2] Troeltsch, *Protestantism and Progress*, pp. 103–04.
[3] *Ibid.*, pp. 192–93.   [4] *Ibid.*, p. 194.   [5] *Ibid.*, p. 195.
[6] *Ibid.*, pp. 204–06.   [7] *Ibid.*, p. 200.   [8] *Ibid.*, pp. 90–91.

control of church policy than do the laymen, illustrates best the institutional weakness of the Protestant churches. Writing of the effect of the democratic structure on the churches, Nottingham said: "If the clergy wish to maintain a position of influence in their own congregations . . . they are almost inevitably driven to compromise or to silence on certain social issues." [9]

Stidley says that this extreme of democracy in religion has caused "diversity nearly to the point of anarchy," for in the overall planning there is a "complete lack of a unified system" and among the welfare agencies there is "almost complete independence." [10]

These conditions are well-illustrated by the experience of the Baptists in their attempts to organize and administer the American Baptist Convention. Because of the importance it assigns to the freedom of the individual, the Baptist church opposes formal organization. According to Baptist theology, all believers possess the full authority of priesthood and any authoritative mediator between the believer and his Creator hinders "free and direct access to the Father." [11] Baptists hold that formal organizational structure interferes with "the free movement of the Holy Spirit." [12]

But Baptists are aware that today this stand as a social policy is archaic. As long ago as the first decade of the present century, Shailer Matthews, the President of the Baptist Convention, said, "The Christian spirit must be institutionalized if it is to prevail in the age of institutions." [13] And there are those today who say that the "pressures of a new social environment" are demanding that Baptists modify their concept of "priesthood of all believers" and "discover a realistic mean between anarchy and hierarchical authority." [14] This modification, however, challenges the Baptist concept of the very nature of the church.

The formation of the American Baptist Convention is one attempt that Baptists have made to institutionalize the Christian spirit,

[9] Nottingham, *Religion and Society*, p. 70.

[10] Stidley, *Sectarian Welfare Federation*, p. 125.

[11] Harrison, *Authority and Power*, p. 56, quoting Edward H. Pruden, *Interpreter Needed*, p. 2.   [12] *Ibid.*, p. 19.

[13] *Ibid.*, p. 54, quoting Shailer Matthews, *The Scientific Management of the Churches*, pp. v–vi.

[14] Harrison, *Authority and Power*, p. 33.

but such authority as the Convention has is delegated upward from the local churches. The congregations that form the Convention retain the right to terminate this authority at any time, since to surrender this right would be a violation of the autonomy of the local church. As a result of his analysis of the Convention, Harrison says that theologically it comes to this:

> God may work through the national boards only if the local churches permit Him to do so. Since He had nothing to do with the creation of these boards, except in an indirect way, He can guide them only through the medium of the local churches.[15]

This puts the executives of the Convention in the middle of a contradiction: responsibility is assigned to them, but legitimate authority is refused them. Lacking true authority, they are forced to assume the power they need to fulfill their responsibility. If by the use of this assumed power they find favor with the Convention, then their power is accorded a fictitious legitimation. In the judgment of Harrison, the result is that the arbitrary legitimizing of power that has not been delegated is precipitating a power struggle at the top of the Convention hierarchy. Hence, there is a contradiction:

> The Baptists, within their system of church-order, have unconsciously created contradictions in order to "preserve pure democracy." It is a contradiction to give to the executives official responsibility but no official authority.[16]

From the executives themselves Harrison learned about the dilemma they face. One said,

> Either someone becomes a dictator and does everything, or plays it safe and does nothing. We believe we have an excuse for doing nothing because Baptist leaders must first discover what the churches want. We'll wait forever! [17]

Another said: " 'I'll tell you the seat of our trouble—autonomy! Everybody is autonomous. We have little dictators all through the Convention!' " [18] Especially where theological matters are involved, policy-makers are frozen into inactivity. One executive said, " 'If

---

[15] *Ibid.*, p. 58.   [16] *Ibid.*, p. 78.   [17] *Ibid.*, p. 116.   [18] *Ibid.*, p. 126.

we started an open discussion on theological issues we'd blow the lid off a boiling pot.' " [19] Harrison concludes that "Executive officials at every level of the denomination are incessantly struggling against the threat of institutional chaos." [20]

Other examples of institutional weakness in specific denominations in the free-church tradition might be cited,[21] but one brief reference to the 1955 Cleveland Conference of the National Council of Churches is telling for the conditions that obtain in many of these denominations. The concluding address of the Executive Secretary of the Department of Social Welfare of the National Council was made before 5,000 delegates. Not even these 5,000, he said, can determine the social-welfare role and function of the churches. They can only be emissaries of good will to the Council's 36 million members, who must ultimately determine welfare policy:

If the church is to be true to its own nature as the great fellowship of all believers in Christ, it is *they* who must determine its role and function. We have made a start. We have democratically involved 5000 people. But there are nearly thirty-six million—that is the challenge before us. No one or two can engineer the policy of the churches; neither can 5000. But together we can involve the church membership all across the land and put before their conscience the need of this generation.[22]

Theological Directions

We have seen that one factor contributing to the weakness of the churches in the area of policy formulation is their organizational weakness. Other theological factors affecting the role of the churches in society have contributed to removing the churches from a more direct involvement in social institutional life.

Randall singles out the separation of moral action from the scheme of salvation ("to divorce the pattern of moral values from that scheme—to make the moral life and its social repercussions

---

[19] *Ibid.*, p. 151.   [20] *Ibid.*, p. 78.

[21] One national executive recently undertook to publish a directory of his church's health and welfare institutions. He traveled around the country and asked the agencies to permit him to list them in the directory. Some of the local ministers and administrators saw in this permission a foreshowing of the first step toward organized authority and diminution of autonomy.

[22] Bachmann, ed., *The Emerging Perspective*, p. 49.

something human and independent") as the most revolutionary revision of the medieval scheme of salvation, for by this cleavage "the
reformers made salvation a purely religious problem, not dependent
at all on human conduct." [23] To remove social morality from the
scheme of salvation was to make religion "nonmoral, a matter of
inner experience and personal attitude, not of conduct" [24] relating
to the social order. With the removal of social morality from the
scheme of salvation, the Protestant churches as institutions were
removed from the world of social injustice and human suffering.

Hence, in the judgment of Limbert, the Protestant churches are
"not regarded as an agency of social control." [25] It must be understood that Limbert here uses the term "social control" in the sense
of control within the framework of the institutional structure of
society. Protestantism seeks to exercise a great deal of control over
individual moral conduct, but most Protestant denominations assume
responsibility for the social character of society only through the
individual.[26] Protestantism's way of fulfilling its social responsibility
is indirect, in Hutchinson's words, "not to offer guidance to society,
but to save individuals." [27] And, in Limbert's, "It is contrary to
Protestant policy . . . to keep control over services relating to the
entire community." [28] The aim of the Protestant churches is not to
build services under church auspices but to create a dedicated and
properly motivated laity, who would develop the services.

Protestant theologians have encouraged this indirect involvement
of the churches in the larger society and in social welfare in particular. In a series of lectures in 1930 on *The Contribution of Religion to Social Work*, Reinhold Niebuhr, directing his attention
to the lack of social justice in the United States, spelled out Protestantism's role in society. He distinguished justice from charity

[23] Randall, "The Churches and the Liberal Tradition," *Annals*, CCLVI
(March, 1948), 149.   [24] *Ibid.*

[25] Paul M. Limbert, "Toward a Protestant Philosophy of Child Welfare," in
Protestant Conference on Child Welfare, *The Nation's Children*, p. 18.

[26] Here again, as in so many contexts, it is impossible to place all Protestant
denominations in one category.

[27] John A. Hutchinson, "Two Decades of Social Christianity," in Hutchinson, ed., *Christian Faith and Social Action*, p. 7.

[28] Limbert, "Toward a Protestant Philosophy of Child Welfare," in Protestant Conference on Child Welfare, *The Nation's Children*, p. 18.

and assigned charity to the churches and justice to the state. To fulfill its responsibility of social justice, he said, the state must institute a program of secularized social work and public welfare. Furthermore, he pointed out certain limitations of sectarian charity and because of these limitations advocated the secularization of social work. Aware of the reaction that this suggestion was likely to trigger in many of his Protestant colleagues, he acknowledged the weakness of Protestantism as a force in society. Desirable or not, the secularization of social work was inevitable because of "the anarchic disunity of Protestantism." [29]

How great has been the influence of these lectures on Protestant welfare policy is clear to anyone who is familiar with those who advocate a similar policy. Their writings contain frequent paraphrases of Niebuhr's statements for the case:

The general tendency of society to take over social services which were once the province of the church, or of some other voluntary agency, is so logical that it might be developed into a principle. The principle is that it is the business of the church and other idealistic institutions to pioneer in the field of social work and to discover obligations which society, as such, has not yet recognized, but to yield these to society as soon as there is a general recognition of society's responsibility thereof.[30]

There is here more than a passion for social justice. Here is a theologian anxious to guard the purity of Protestant theology. In 1907, when the answers to social problems were called "gospel," a Baptist minister, Edward Judson, cautioned the churches against an inapt involvement in social action:

Social problems are so difficult and so fascinating that they easily absorb all a minister's time and energy. He neglects his study and the care of his flock. He loses his priestly character and becomes a mere social functionary.[31]

The social-gospel movement was a reaction against the exaggerated spiritualism and the pietistic individualism that had been so largely responsible for the churches' removal from the field of

---

[29] Reinhold Niebuhr, *The Contribution of Religion to Social Work*, p. 15.
[30] *Ibid.*, pp. 16–17.
[31] Judson, "The Church in Its Social Aspect," *Annals*, XXX, No. 3 (November, 1907), 9.

social action. The aim of this new gospel was to reawaken the churches to their responsibility for the social order. For a time it was popular and even gained some momentum, until it was challenged by the fundamentalists, who feared that it would lead to the Christian gospel being identified with the reconstruction of society.[32] Theologians are more alert than are laymen to the almost imperceptible ways by which theology can be transformed into social work.[33] Protestant theologians were still convinced that salvation was a purely religious problem,[34] requiring no direct involvement in social action, and they advised church-related welfare agencies that the secularization of their services was "a desirable end." [35]

In 1930 Mary Richmond, writing of the secularization of services, pointed up the churches' indirect involvement in social action: "The Church furnishes us with the motive for all our work, it heartens us . . . and sends us forward on life's battlefield to do our allotted part in a campaign that involves wider issues." [36] This philosophy of indirect participation in social action was expounded and elaborated in the many writings of F. Ernest Johnson:

> It is my conviction that the conduct of social services by the church, broadly speaking, is not the normal expression of Christian social motive. As the institution pre-eminently responsible for the teaching of ideals and attitudes, keeping faith alive and inspiring to high endeavor, the church can function best by impregnating social work and all other community functions with its purpose, its vision, and its courage.[37]

At the 1961 National Conference on the Churches and Social

---

[32] Mead, "American Protestantism since the Civil War," *Journal of Religion*, XXXVI, No. 2 (April, 1956), 84–86.

[33] France a little more than a decade ago is a case in point. The priest-worker movement put upon the priest a double role. The components of a double role are not always incompatible, but in this case the double role was evidently too demanding. Sanctioned by some of the French bishops, the movement was permitted for a while, but eventually ecclesiastical sanction was withdrawn.

[34] Randall, "The Churches and the Liberal Tradition," *Annals*, CCLVI (1948), 149.

[35] Reinhold Niebuhr, *The Contribution of Religion to Social Work*, p. 15.

[36] Richmond, *The Long View*, p. 115.

[37] F. Ernest Johnson, *The Church and Society*, p. 145.

Welfare, sponsored by the National Council of Churches, Haskell Miller of the Wesley Theological Seminary exhorted the delegates to adhere to this indirect involvement of the churches in welfare: "Government is the means which a free people use to get their needs met in the most comprehensive and meaningful way possible." [38] He also defined the role of the churches:

The Protestant churches of America should lay claim to Protestantism's central, historic social welfare emphasis. This emphasis is, as I see it, on the responsibility of the total society to make responsible provision, primarily through agencies of amenable government, for the security and welfare of all persons in the community life.[39]

This is apparently the role of the church in welfare that many, perhaps most, Protestants accept in practice. A former dean of a school of social work couched the rationale of this role in terms of the church's resources and its primary responsibility:

When the church diverts its limited money, personnel and attention to things that are generally enough accepted that government funds are available for them, will it have sufficient resources for its *unique* responsibility? I doubt it.[40]

The function of the church is the formation of the Christian conscience; to other social institutions, preeminent among which is the state, belongs the function of social welfare. The church should not spread its limited resources so thin but should "concentrate its attention upon what it is uniquely equipped to do." [41]

Societal Influences

In addition to these two factors within Protestantism—its organizational weakness, which rendered policy-making difficult, and the sanctions of its theologians, who advised against direct involvement with the machinery of society—there is a third factor, external to church structure and theology, which contributed further and significantly to the weakening and the minimizing of the churches'

---

[38] Miller, "Government's Role in Social Welfare," p. 6.   [39] *Ibid.,* p. 9.
[40] Letter from Donald S. Howard to the director of the Department of Social Welfare of the National Council of the Churches of Christ in the U.S.A., April 2, 1959.   [41] *Ibid.*

role in society, particularly their role in social welfare. This third factor was the dominance of Protestantism in America during the rise and development of welfare services. This dominance made it unnecessary for the churches to make a conscious effort to participate in direct welfare services, and they automatically assumed an individualistic laissez-faire attitude about their own welfare role. Perhaps the elements in this third factor have been overstressed and other theological reasons lost sight of; nevertheless, this third factor bears discussion here.

In a pluralistic society a minority group feels the need to maintain as a bulwark against the encroachment of the value system of the majority group its own institutions with their value orientation. A majority group, however, does not need such a bulwark to assure the preservation of its way of life, since its values are reflected in the patterns and policies of the larger society.[42] At one time American society was practically identical with Protestant society. Social institutions reflected Protestant values, and in the field of welfare agency, staffs and boards of directors were frequently also lay trustees of Protestant churches. Nonsectarian social work was therefore bound to reflect Protestant values, and it was easy for Protestants to adjust to secularization in social welfare, as they had done in education.[43] Welfare agencies, public and private, reflected the prevailing religious culture, Protestantism, and were at the same time channels of Christian benevolence through which the Protestant churches influenced society.[44]

Catholics and Jews, however, both minority groups, felt the need for their own value systems within the context of the Protestant system. Evidence for this need among Catholics is seen in the benevolent societies that had their origins along the eastern seaboard and whose purpose was to help Catholic immigrants who overnight found themselves in a foreign milieu.

What was for many Catholic immigrants a social necessity was

---

[42] F. Ernest Johnson, "Protestant Social Work," in Kurtz, ed., *Social Work Year Book 1954*, p. 378.

[43] Cayton and Nishi, eds., *The Changing Scene*, p. 59.

[44] F. Ernest Johnson, "Reflection and Perspective," in F. Ernest Johnson, ed., *Religion and Social Work*, p. 179.

no less necessary for Jewish immigrants. In fact, it is not unlikely that the provision of welfare services was imposed upon the Jews from their first entrance into the New World. Shortly after the first 23 Jews landed in New Amsterdam in 1654, Governor Stuyvesant, fearing that their indigence would make them a public charge, wrote to the West India Company for authorization to banish them. The reply of the company was a conditional permission for the Jews to remain: " 'provided the poor among them shall not become a burden . . . but be supported by their own nation.' " [45]

In general, Protestant society had no similar need for such subcultural structures; but today, when society is no longer Protestant but pluralistic, leaders in Protestant welfare are demanding, as we shall see below, more specifically Protestant church-related services.

A Changing Policy

The caution of Judson and the advice and prediction of Niebuhr seem to many to be unrealistic. A theology that is overprotected against the world and that relegates religion to the task of saving souls apart from any direct involvement in the social order can be unwise as a basis for social policy. According to Hutchinson, this policy has wrought a twofold tragedy, religious and moral:

The religious tragedy is that such religion fails utterly to bring any of our life, individual or social, under the perspective of biblical religion. . . . The moral tragedy is that it affords no principle of social judgment whereby American interest or values may be realistically appraised and evaluated.[46]

Protestants are aware of this double tragedy. There are many welfare agencies and other social institutions which trace their origins to Protestant churches but which today are no longer church-affiliated and retain few if any vestiges of Protestantism. Although they grew up out of the church, they have been trans-

---

[45] William Avrunin, "Jewish Social Services," in Kurtz, ed., *Social Work Year Book 1957*, p. 324. Although this incident is frequently cited in social welfare sources, Israel S. Chipkin discredits it as "legend" in his "Judaism and Social Welfare," in Finkelstein, ed., *The Jews*, II, 1052.

[46] Hutchinson, ed., *Christian Faith and Social Action*, p. 7.

formed into nonsectarian institutions, according to the principle of Niebuhr. The professional practices of these agencies are frequently based on a secular concept of the nature of man and society, and Protestant leaders recognize that their policies exclude "religion in any form except the most generalized of naturalistic and humanistic tenets." [47] The research report presented to the Cleveland Conference of the National Council of Churches underscored the trend to secularization even in minute particulars:

> If a boy's worker wishes to invite a child to Sunday school, such invitation must be personal and even surreptitious; it must not be public in a group of mixed religious composition; and above all it must not be mentioned in the annual request for support from the community chest.[48]

The churches are questioning the motivation of their policy, whether it might not have been a way to avoid responsibility. Many Protestants therefore want a reevaluation of the policy. "It may well be time to re-examine honestly a philosophy which, however noble in purpose, seems to provide an excuse for the evasion of responsibility." [49] At recent conferences many have voiced the obligation of the churches to participate directly in social services—as many insisted several years ago on the obligation of the churches to participate only indirectly.

The 1954 *Social Work Year Book* stated that formerly Protestants "could adjust themselves to the passing over of social work to secular, nonsectarian auspices, in the same fashion as they did with respect to the secularization of education." [50] More recently, however, the Protestant pattern of thought and action has indicated a desire to expand direct services under the control of the churches. Compare the 1954 statement with the following from the 1957 *Social Work Year Book:* "There is in evidence a disposition to make Protestant social work a more distinct entity than it has been in the past." [51] There is less and less talk of motivating the individual apart

---

[47] Cayton and Nishi, eds., *The Changing Scene*, p. 138.
[48] *Ibid.*, p. 139.   [49] *Ibid.*, p. 151.
[50] F. Ernest Johnson, "Protestant Social Work," in Kurtz, ed., *Social Work Year Book 1954*, p. 378.
[51] F. Ernest Johnson and William J. Villaume, "Protestant Social Services," in Kurtz, ed., *Social Work Year Book 1957*, p. 423.

from social action and more talk of an extensive church-related welfare program:

The role and function of Protestant social services are under consideration in the American churches. Although Protestants continue actively to support nonsectarian community services and frequently speak of the expansion of public services, many church leaders feel the maintenance of Protestant social services are a necessary expression of the churches' concern for the welfare of the whole man, especially in view of the growth of Protestant church membership among the less privileged.[52]

Even some Protestant theologians have recently advised the direct involvement of the churches in welfare services, thus reversing the earlier theological sanctions. Notwithstanding Protestant theology's traditional separation of moral action from the scheme of salvation and its heavy emphasis on man's sinful nature, some theologians are calling to the attention of the churches the "divine imperative to do what little a sinful 'creature' can to be like his Creator."[53] And Protestants are rising to this challenge. Church welfare executives agree that a welfare system based on a philosophy of "ethical humanitarianism" alone is inadequate.[54] Addressing the delegates at the Lutheran Conference in Ohio, the General Secretary of the Oslo Innermission Church of Norway said: "The welfare state can never replace Christian charity," and the churches may not therefore "write off the responsibility for Christian service to the welfare state."[55] Bachmann has summarized the recent thinking of Protestant churchmen:

Within the past decades there has been a growing concern on the part of many churchmen, clergy and laity alike, that the increasing secularization of the welfare services . . . has just about left religion out. Therefore there are denominational leaders . . . who feel that the time may have arrived when the church, which was the originator of most modern social work, must reassert itself, and reclaim some of the ground it has lost.[56]

[52] *Ibid.*
[53] Arthur L. Swift, Jr., "The Church and Human Welfare," in F. Ernest Johnson, ed., *Religion and Social Work*, pp. 8–9.
[54] Bachmann, ed., *The Activating Concern*, p. 2.
[55] Rev. Andreas Grasmo, "The Methods and Resources Available to the Church in Providing Responsible Service to People," in National Lutheran Council, *Christ Frees and Unites*, p. 51.
[56] Bachmann, ed., *The Activating Concern*, pp. 119–20.

It would be an oversimplification to say that this trend among Protestant theologians and welfare executives has free rein and is not countered by Protestant leaders who see the role of the church as being directly related only to the individual. Some Protestants still maintain that the spiritual character of the church should be so emphasized as to exclude a direct social welfare function, which, they continue to hold, should be relegated to other social institutions. Nevertheless, there are three areas related to the three factors discussed above in which Protestant activities are showing marked signs of a new attitude toward the church's role in social welfare.

The first area is policy-making. The churches are aware that their individualistic structure makes difficult the formation of social policy. For some of the churches the difficulties are more extreme than for others, but all recognize the necessity for greater organizational cohesion if the church is to play a more significant role in modern institutional life.

The second area is direct social responsibility. The transformation of the American socio-religious culture from Protestant to pluralistic is for sociological reasons forcing the churches to assume direct responsibility for and control of their own welfare services.

The third area is the relationship of the scheme of salvation to social action. Churchmen, many of them theologians holding executive welfare positions, are coming to interpret the concept of *diakonia* as a balance of word and work, active faith and love, by which the churches must assume direct responsibility for the individual and for the social institutions and agencies in which he participates.

CATHOLICISM

Students of religious sociology are aware of the difference between Protestantism and Catholicism as institutions of social control. In general, the social function of Protestantism has been the direct control of the moral conduct of the individual and, in the hope that he will then mold the institutions of society to the Christian conscience, the indirect control of society. Catholic social philosophy has always aimed toward more than the motivation of individuals, with the hope that they will then mold the institutions of society to the Christian conscience. Its policies aim toward a more direct influence upon the institutional forms of society. Catholic theology considers that the church has a universal and transcendental mission and that every element in the social structure partakes of that transcendentalism. This means that all human affairs—art, science, humanism, the institutions of the social structure—partake of the transcendental teleology of the church. And this is the basis of the church's involvement in the world.[57]

Organizational Structure

The social structure of the Catholic church is geared to this transcendental mission. It is an episcopal type of institution, authority proceeding from the top. The hierarchical structure of the church permits autonomy in many areas, but in matters of faith and morality, papal and episcopal authority do not depend upon delegation from local churches. From the point of view of organizational structure and social function, it is instructive to compare a Protestant's and a Catholic's definition of the church—the classic definitions of Luther and of Bellarmine. Luther's definition is "A spiritual assembly of souls in one faith. . . . The true, real, right, essential Church is a spiritual thing, and not anything external or outward." [58] Bellarmine's definition is "A union of men who profess the same Christian faith and participate in the same sacraments, under the dominion of legitimate pastors and especially of the one Vicar of Christ on earth." [59]

These definitions are most sharply contrasted by their separate social-control terminology: "spiritual assembly . . . not external or outward" in one, "union . . . dominion of legitimate pastors . . .

---

[57] Speaking, not within a theological, but within a sociological frame of reference, Yinger sees somewhat differently the church's transcendental mission: "Its strategy is not to let science, rationalism, humanism, or whatnot independently accomplish anything if the church can possibly step in to show that the new development is really a fundamental and established part of the church program." See his *Religion in the Struggle for Power*, p. 43.

[58] *Works of Martin Luther*, the Philadelphia edition (Philadelphia, Muhlenberg Press, 1943), I, 353–54. [59] Robert Bellarmine, *De Ecclesia* III, 2, 9.

Vicar" in the other. Had Max Weber antedated Bellarmine, Bellarmine's definition of the church might have been chosen from the sociologist's pages on orders of legitimation, dominion, and structures of dominancy.

Sociologically speaking, a hierarchically structured church is at a greater advantage in a bureaucratic society than it is in an individualistic society. In an individualistic society the Catholic church encounters difficulties because many of its administrative principles run counter to many of the principles of individualism, but in a collectivist society the Catholic church is less endangered by the power struggle than are more loosely knit groups. The unity of the Catholic church makes it more resistant to the growing power of modern bureaucracies. Perhaps for this reason Catholicism is less fearful than is Protestantism that financial or other involvement with the state will endanger its mission.

The disparity between the resistance power of Catholicism and that of Protestantism is recognized. According to Glock, those characteristics of the Catholic church that render it more resistant to the power struggle—organizational structure, ideological unity, and ability to present a relatively united point of view on most issues—cause a certain amount of concern to Protestants.[60] These are characteristics which much of Protestant theology renders impossible to the Protestant churches.

Theology and Policy

In keeping with its theology of the transcendental nature of the church, Catholicism sees as proper to its mission a direct involvement of the church in the social order. That the church encourages detachment from the world is not considered an excuse for disengagement from the world's problems, for since human life is essentially a relationship between persons, a social relationship, the perfection of that relationship is the perfection of the social order with its social institutions. Therefore, in order to perfect the social insti-

[60] Glock, "Issues That Divide," *Journal of Social Issues*, XII, No. 3 (1956), 41–42.

tutions in which men participate, the church must be directly involved with social action.

It is argued that the social order is perfected through social justice, which is the work of the state. In the Catholic view, however, the social order depends upon charity as well as justice. Social justice alone is insufficient. Without charity "the technique of politics and economics will not be able to do more than tinker with the social machine; it cannot make it run." [61] This is not to say that charity is a substitute for social justice. Justice regulates the relations between men as possessors; charity regulates the relations between men as persons. "Unless the relation between men as persons is regulated . . . their relations as possessors will always be snarled." [62] The perfection of the social order is based on social justice but "informed by the spirit of social charity and the solidarity of all men." The social role of the church, therefore, is to achieve this perfection of men and the social order by becoming part of the "grimy machinery of society." [63]

Unlike many of the Protestant churches, whose policies are geared to indirect involvement in social action, the Catholic church sees the necessity for direct involvement if the social order is to be based on social justice infused with charity.

Social Philosophy

The social philosophy principle that is generally accepted by Catholics as primary in governing the relations between social institutions both voluntary and governmental is the principle of subsidiarity. Though not derived from Catholic dogma, subsidiarity is compatible with it.

The principle of subsidiarity presupposes the organic structure of society, the total social system comprising various levels and groups —primary, secondary, tertiary. Through these more and less intimate associations individuals find fullness of social relationship, and the entire social system is enriched thereby. As in a biological or-

[61] Murray, "Roman Catholic Church," *Annals*, CCLVI (1948), 42.
[62] *Ibid.*   [63] *Ibid.*, p. 39.

ganism, each group both fulfills its own end and functions for the well-being of society as a whole.[64]

By the principle of subsidiarity is meant that each of these various levels of associations is autonomous within the limits of its social function. Higher and more powerful associations should not assume the responsibility or embrace the functions of minor associations that are able to carry their own responsibilities and fulfill their own functions. The word *subsidiary* means "giving help." Applied to relationships between government and voluntary agencies, the principle prescribes that where a voluntary association is wholly unequal to its task, the agency must relinquish the task. Where, however, the voluntary association can with help fulfill its responsibility and function, government should extend enabling assistance. Applied in this way, the principle is one of self-determination on the societal level. When, however, government chooses not to give enabling assistance and to take to itself unnecessarily the responsibility and function of such an association, it not only overburdens itself with functions for which it is not equipped, but it also deprives individuals of their right to and need for voluntary association.[65]

According to Maritain, the principle of subsidiarity is basic to a sound social philosophy. Government should, he says, "leave to the multifarious organs of the social body the autonomous initiative and management of all the activities which by nature pertain to them." [66]

This principle has been widely recognized since the publication of Pius XI's encyclical "Quadragesimo Anno." "It is indeed true," wrote the Pontiff, ". . . that owing to the change in social conditions, much that was formerly done by small bodies can nowadays be accomplished only by large corporations"; [67] but he cautioned against a new social structure in which everything would be indiscriminately regarded as the direct responsibility of government:

Just as it is wrong to withdraw from the individual and commit to the community at large what private enterprise and industry can accomplish, so, too, it is an injustice, a grave evil and a disturbance of right

[64] Gordon, *Security, Freedom and Happiness*, p. 150.
[65] *Ibid.*, pp. 149–50.   [66] Maritain, *Man and the State*, p. 23.
[67] Pius XI, "Quadragesimo Anno," in *Five Great Encyclicals*, p. 147, par. 79.

order for a larger and higher organization to arrogate to itself functions which can be performed efficiently by smaller and lower bodies. This is a fundamental principle of social philosophy, unshaken and unchangeable.[68]

Pius XI pointed out the good that would accrue to society by the application of this principle:

The more faithfully this principle be followed, and a graded hierarchical order exist between the various subsidiary organizations, the more excellent will be both the authority and the efficiency of the social organization as a whole.[69]

In the United States Catholic bishops and welfare executives have applied the principle of subsidiarity to welfare. Fearing the principle was being ignored, the bishops have spoken out against the trend in this country for more and more welfare to be brought within the exclusive province of government.[70] This is the philosophy that guides the policies of Catholic welfare executives, as recently voiced by Msgr. Raymond Gallagher, Secretary of the National Conference of Catholic Charities:

Ideally, each individual should be able to take care of himself. When this is impossible he looks to the members of his immediate family for assistance. When these resources are insufficient he looks to typical citizen organizations such as religious, civic, and patriotic groups. When all of these voluntary groups are unable to meet the problem, then the lowest echelon of government should be required to meet the need. Similar respect for the prior rights of the lower echelons of government is expected according to this principle.[71]

According to this social philosophy, society through the state will put at the disposal of voluntary associations "such resources as will enable them to continue their proper function in society." [72] This assistance can take various forms and be made available in various degrees:

The initial method would be for the government to encourage and stimulate the lower groups of society to meet their own needs . . . through the

---

[68] *Ibid.*   [69] *Ibid.*, par. 80.
[70] "The Child: Citizen of Two Worlds," in *Our Bishops Speak*, p. 164.
[71] Gallagher, "The Place of Government in Welfare," pp. 4–5.
[72] Guilfoyle, "The Role of Public Welfare," p. 7.

enabling grant of government funds and facilities. This co-sharing with the lower groups preserves their own responsibilities for self help. . . . There would be varying ascending degrees of government's role from this initial one right up to a situation wherein the facts would be such that government would be forced to take over certain areas of need directly and completely.[73]

The Catholic church, therefore, regards government as an auxiliary in the performing of welfare functions. Speaking of the role of church and state in welfare, Msgr. Gallagher said, "Government is cast in the role of an 'enabler.' " Within the government structure this means that the Federal government provides only those things that are necessary to enable lower echelons of government to perform the task at hand. Msgr. Gallagher sees the same principle as applying to voluntary welfare effort: "To extend this principle of enabling to churches from the Federal Government does not seem to us to destroy the proper relationship of government to private citizen organizations." [74]

To some this principle seems too conservative and not serviceable in a modern welfare society, where the need is for increasing government action. The Catholic answer to these objections is that the principle is a social one. That the principle is relative and not absolute makes it flexible. It can be applied variously in various societies and under different circumstances and hence can be highly serviceable as a principle of social policy.

Depending on their liberal or conservative political leanings, Catholics throughout the world differ on the application of the principle of subsidiarity. The Catholic Social Guild in England is a case in point. The Guild, whose leaders are priests, is a study and social action group interested in the changing social order. The social philosophy of the movement is that of an organic-structured society dominated by the principle of subsidiarity. Recently Ryan made a study of its membership to determine the Guild's attitude on the English welfare state. The study revealed a diversity of opinion about the application of the principle that runs the gamut

[73] *Ibid.*
[74] Letter to the author from Msgr. Gallagher, February 13, 1961.

from conservative to liberal. The following is a summary of the findings of the study:

The truth is that the Guild as a body has no unified opinion on the Welfare State. Opinions of both leaders and members vary all the way from unconditional support to outright condemnation of this new British institution.[75]

1329479

JUDAISM

The focus of the matter changes when one passes from the social role of the Christian churches to that of the Jews. Although Protestants and Catholics differ about methods of social action, both are coming more and more to regard their social role as endowing social institutions and society as a whole with transcendental values. Hence, Catholicism and much of Protestantism, as social institutions, aim at the elimination of secularism and the reflection of religious culture in the social structure. While it is impossible to state one view that would characterize all Jewish groups, it may be said that for many Jews social action is directed toward achieving a secular society, and toward the maintaining of secular institutions.

Two related social phenomena condition the social role of Judaism. There is the secular-religious conflict between Jews and Christians, and there is the split in American Judaism between Jewish religious and nonreligious institutions.

Sacred-Secular Conflict

The relative position of the Jewish community today is similar to that of the Catholic community a century ago. A century ago Catholics felt threatened by a Protestant society; today Jews feel a similar threat from the Christian society. Herberg states the Jewish anxiety bluntly:

Because the western Jew achieved emancipation with the secularization of society, he can preserve his free and equal status only so long as culture and society remain secular. But let religion gain a significant place

[75] Ryan, "C.S.G. and the Welfare State," *Social Order*, V, No. 6 (June, 1955), 270.

in the everyday life of the community, and the Jew because he is outside the bounds of the dominant religion, will once again be relegated to the margins of society, displaced, disfranchised culturally if not politically, shorn of rights and opportunities.[76]

Only in the light of this anxiety can we understand the Jews' interest in civil rights and their advocacy of a wide separation of church and state.[77] Kertzer's statement explains the affinity of some Jewish organizations for the ultraconservative POAU:

The First Amendment to the American Constitution, interpreted by Jefferson as establishing a wall of separation, has been the modern Magna Carta of New World Jewry—our guarantee that we will never be second-class citizens. That is why we Jews embrace it so fondly.[78]

To many Americans this anxiety is difficult to understand. Even some Jews admit that "there is a pathological element in our fears," [79] but history reminds them of other times when Christians showed "no sensitivity to Jewish feelings." [80] And modern times are not too comforting. If in recent history both Catholics and Protestants have had amicable experiences in their relations with the state, the same cannot be said for Jews: "Among Jews there has been no modern record of a happy mating of religion and State." [81]

Hence, many Jews see in a secular state a means by which the Jewish community can be maintained on an equal footing with other religious groups. A secular state and society is a guarantee of the removal from public institutions of all that is socially, legally, and culturally Christian. While many Jews would reject his prin-ciple, many accept Pfeffer's expression of the social ideal of this country: "Normality in American culture is secularity." [82] The dominant American tradition, the "public ethos," is "libertarian,

---

[76] Herberg, *Protestant, Catholic, Jew*, p. 239.

[77] A Jewish student in attendance at a lecture given by the author tersely summarized the reason for Jewish anxiety and the affinity of some Jewish organizations for the Protestants and Other Americans United for the Sepa-ration of Church and State (POAU): "Once separation of church and state goes, the Jew will be low man on the totem pole."

[78] Kertzer, "Religions in a Democratic Society," *Reconstructionist*, XXV, No. 1 (February 20, 1959), 6.

[79] *Ibid.*   [80] *Ibid.*   [81] *Ibid.*

[82] Pfeffer, "Changing Relationships among Religious Groups," *Journal of Intergroup Relations*, I, No. 2 (Spring, 1960), 88.

humanist, and secular," [83] but this statement does not mean that the American people are without religion: "We are a religious people, but our government is religionless." [84] Arthur Gilbert, the Associate Editor of the *Reconstructionist*, has expressed a similar view:

For many Jews a secularized America is more comfortable than a "Christianized" America. In a secular America we may, to paraphrase the poet, be Jews in our tents and Americans in society without conflict. But if American society expresses itself through Christian symbols, there will be a tension between our loyalties to our Judaism and our Americanism.[85]

Jewish advocates of secularization recognize that their attitude is shocking to Catholics and Protestants and even to some Jews.[86] Gilbert sees both Catholics and Protestants recoiling from the substitution of Americanism for Christianity, and Protestants especially he sees anxious "to reassert and redefine the sectarian sources of the values of our culture." [87] Most Protestants and Catholics do not accept the thesis that a secular society can be friendly to religion. Bishop Herntrich stated the case flatly: mere "humanistic systems take on anti-humanistic tendencies." [88] Segments of the Jewish community recognize this, and among them is observable a trend to reject proponents of a secularistic society as not representative of the Jewish community.[89] But this creates a conflict. In the words of Gilbert:

We have fallen back upon the rational arguments of the secularist and

[83] *Ibid.*, p. 93.

[84] Leo Pfeffer, in National Conference of Christians and Jews, *The Nature of Religious Pluralism.*

[85] Gilbert, "Religion and the Free Society," *Reconstructionist*, XXIV, No. 11 (October 3, 1958), 12.   [86] *Ibid.*   [87] *Ibid.*, p. 11.

[88] Bishop D. Volkmar Herntrich, "The Nature of Man and His Destiny According to the Christian Faith," in National Lutheran Council, *Christ Frees and Unites*, p. 41.

[89] Gilbert, "Religion and the Free Society," *Reconstructionist*, XXIV, No. 11 (October 3, 1958), 11. Gilbert's article is an account and commentary on the dialogue sponsored by the Fund for the Republic in the spring of 1958. Among the participants in the dialogue were Leo Pfeffer and Will Herberg. Pfeffer is a separationist; Herberg advocates tax support even for sectarian education. In Gilbert's judgment neither is truly representative of the Jewish community. Pfeffer, he says, does not identify with any philosophy of Judaism, nor does he relate the problem of church-state separation to any Jewish philosophy. Herberg, on the other hand, has little identification with Jewish anxieties in American society.

the prudential judgments of the pragmatist and so we have provoked queries from Protestants and Catholics who want to know why and how on *religious* grounds can we, a religious people, defend a thesis that would remove all reference to God from society and from our political institutions.[90]

In 1962 the conflict was illustrated in the dialogue among Jews following the Supreme Court's rule barring the use of the Regents Prayer in New York State public schools. The American Jewish Committee and the Anti-Defamation League of B'nai B'rith filed an *amici curiae* brief in connection with public school prayer cases in Maryland and Pennsylvania, and almost simultaneously a leader in Orthodox Jewry, Rabbi Menachem M. Schneerson, urged the reversal of the Supreme Court's ruling. Rabbi Schneerson stated: "With the exception of a small number of secularists and atheists, there is no parent who could in all conscience object to a nondenominational prayer per se." [91] Perhaps even more startling was the resolution by the Jewish Orthodox Union not to oppose Federal aid to religious schools. By the resolution the Union abandoned a position that it had held for ten years to oppose Federal aid.[92]

These are signs that the Jewish community is awakening to the need for rethinking Jewish theology and social philosophy and becoming involved in the work of applying policies derived therefrom to American social issues.[93] Many recent publications, conferences, and discussions center around definitions and components of Jewishness and are geared to the integration of the religious, cultural, and historical aspects of the Jewish people and the relations of these factors to social welfare policy.

Religious and Nonreligious Institutions

The other aspect of the social role of Judaism concerns the division between religious and nonreligious institutions. Anyone only slightly acquainted with sectarian social welfare knows the long

---

[90] *Ibid.*, p. 12.
[91] *Catholic Messenger*, December 6, 1962, p. 8.   [92] *Ibid.*
[93] Gilbert, "Religion and the Free Society," *Reconstructionist*, XXIV (October 3, 1958), 11.

religious roots that nourish Jewish welfare services. These roots go back to Deuteronomy, where God commanded charity:

When you reap your harvest in your field, and forget a sheaf in the field, you must not go back to get it; it is to go to the resident alien, the orphan, and the widow. . . . When you beat your olive trees, you must not go over them a second time; that is to go to the resident alien, the orphan, and the widow. . . . When you pick the grapes of your vineyard, you must not go over it a second time; that is to go to the resident alien, the orphan, and the widow.[94]

The religious roots of Jewish welfare were recrystallized in the frequently quoted Eight Degrees of Charity of Maimonides. These degrees proceed from the first stage, where one gives grudgingly and reluctantly; higher in the scale are giving unasked and giving without knowing to whom one gives. The highest degree of charity is to help a fellow man achieve self-support. The term used by the Jews to express this concept is *zedakah*, which is probably best translated by "social justice." *Zedakah* is a social obligation of the entire community, it not being left to the individual's judgment. This is the root of the socio-religious character of Jewish welfare and explains why Jewish welfare institutions were originally closely associated not only with the Jewish religion and the rabbinical groups but with the synagogue itself.

In modern times, however, there have been some significant changes in the pattern of Jewish welfare. The primary instruments of welfare services as well as other social action programs among Jews are not the rabbinical groups but Jewish welfare associations and civil rights groups which, although they may retain some thin affiliation with the synagogue and the various religious communities, are generally separate from them and independent. Several factors contributed to the separation. Because Jewish immigrants were from culturally different European backgrounds, the various cultural groups, even though they attended the same synagogue, were inclined to establish their separate welfare services, which were generally unified in a community center. Perhaps a more significant influence came from the religious diversity within Judaism in the United States.

[94] Deuteronomy XXIV, 19–21.

More than a century ago in this country, therefore, Jews found in their welfare institutions a source of unity that no longer existed in their synagogues. The synagogue continued to lose importance as a social institution until "by the end of the Civil War, the synagogue had ceased to be the central power in the communal life." [95] Thus, the welfare institution and the federation came to be not only the main instrument of social action but more especially "a vehicle of social prestige." [96]

Such a development has had at least one significant consequence. Aside from its influence on the individual lives of Jews—and in many instances it exerts a strongly positive influence—the Jewish religion as an institutionalized instrument of social control has diminished with this separation of Jewish welfare institutions from the synagogue. It is not clear whether the influence of the Jewish religion diminished as a result of the separate growth and strength of Jewish welfare institutions or whether separate welfare institutions grew in importance because of the diminishing significance of the Jewish religion. At any rate, it is the Jewish welfare institution that fulfills "the desire of Jews to live as Jews and to have a communal life and certain institutional forms of their own." [97] Among Jewish welfare agencies "there is limited evidence of Jewish content in casework practice." [98]

Kutzik's thesis is even more bold: "Jewish agencies have not only been unable significantly to help bring about positive Jewish attitudes in their clients but have even failed to do so in their staffs." [99] It is not surprising that Kutzik's thesis was contested from several

---

[95] Herman D. Stein, "Jewish Social Work in the United States (1654–1954)," in *American Jewish Yearbook 1956*, p. 13.   [96] *Ibid.*

[97] Avrunin, "Jewish Social Services," in Kurtz, ed., *Social Work Year Book 1957*, p. 326, quoting a statement of a committee of the Council of Jewish Federations and Welfare Funds.   [98] *Ibid.*, p. 326.

[99] Kutzik, *Social Work and Jewish Values*, p. 5. Kutzik's thesis is stronger than that enunciated above. He holds that in Jewish agencies generally there exists an "unresolved conflict—*a conflict between certain basic Jewish values and certain basic social work values*" (p. 6) and that this conflict will be resolved only when Jewish social workers resolve "the major conflict between their professional and personal selves *by recognizing and rejecting those Jewish values in conflict with social work and buttressing their social work values with consonant Jewish ones*" (pp. 6–7).

quarters. Whatever evidence may exist for or against this thesis, many if not most Jewish social workers recognize that while their agencies are carriers of many elements of Jewish culture, they lack a vigorous identification with the Jewish religion.

The pattern, therefore, of Jewish welfare services differs considerably from that of Protestant and Catholic services. Protestant and Catholic services are under the auspices and organization of the church; Jewish services are free from the direction of the synagogue and temple. Some Jewish welfare executives do not consider that this arrangement has resulted in the secularization of the Jewish services; they regard the historical roots and primordial religious motivation as still an energizing influence in spite of the organizational separation of welfare programs from the synagogue. Others, however, admit to a secularization of the Jewish services, and lament it. In the judgment of some rabbis it has "robbed the community of a large reservoir of interest and energy and support in the social field." [100]

No statement can be made to cover all Jews or even the three rabbinical groups, but in the thinking of Orthodox Jews especially this divorce of the religious community from the welfare community is to be deplored. To quote one Orthodox rabbi: "The failure of leaders to appreciate the importance of the function of the synagogue in the social field, their endeavor to exclude it from participation in social work and community service, is difficult to understand." [101] Those who regard the Jewish religion as the core of Jewish life and culture are chagrined when they read statements like the following: "Jewish communal agencies are today essentially secular institutions. . . . The modern rabbi is thought of as only one among professional Jewish workers." [102] This chagrin is deepened when they hear it charged that many Jewish social workers and executives are opposed to sectarian agencies and are even hostile to the synagogues. [103]

Whatever may be the present degree of secularization of the

[100] Goldstein, *The Synagogue and Social Welfare*, p. 52.   [101] *Ibid.*
[102] Alter F. Landesman, "Jewish Social Work Today," in F. Ernest Johnson, ed., *Religion and Social Work*, p. 68.
[103] Goldstein, *The Synagogue and Social Welfare*, p. 52.

Jewish agencies by reason of their separation from the synagogue and temple, there are at least beginnings of a movement toward a closer relationship between the welfare and the religious communities. In recent years there have been from various quarters proposals that the synagogue and the community services move toward a closer relationship and reestablish the former integration of synagogue and welfare services. There are isolated examples of welfare agencies functioning under the leadership of rabbis.

Much of the impetus toward this end comes from rabbis who are alerting welfare directors to their responsibility to preserve Jewish values and are reminding them that foremost in the concept of Jewishness is dedication to Jewish religious values. Rabbi Jacob Weinstein scored the disregard for these values in other facets of Jewish life: "Attempts to extract the culture or the peoplehood from the religion have succeeded only in providing a desiccated literature and a brittle nationalism." [104] Allowing that diversity of religious affiliation among Jews augments the problem of informing communal services with Jewish religious values, Rabbi Weinstein suggested that social workers identify themselves with "that phase of Judaism which is most congenial to them and work through the democratic processes of the Synagogue." [105] Thus, recent Jewish welfare conferences and Jewish welfare literature seem to be following this trend. Efforts are being made to identify specific Jewish values and to map out procedures by which these values may be instilled in the Jewish agencies.[106]

CONCLUSIONS

From the foregoing analysis of the role conception the churches have of themselves as social institutions the following broad conclusions may be drawn:

The three religious groups have different conceptions of their role in society and in social welfare.

Among the Protestant churches there is a broad range of social

[104] Weinstein, "Responsibility of Jewish Community Services," *Journal of Jewish Communal Services*, XXXV, No. 1 (Fall, 1958), 33.
[105] *Ibid.*   [106] Landesman, *Religion and Social Work*, p. 68.

philosophies stemming from the theological divergences among the churches. In general, however, the Protestant churches have conceived their role in the social order as an indirect one which aims at sanctifying and motivating the individual, who then bears responsibility for molding society to a pattern amenable to the Christian conscience.

There are, however, definite indications that the Protestant policy of indirect involvement in the social order is being changed for a policy of more direct action affecting the pattern of social institutions and for a policy that would directly commit the Protestant churches to a full-scale pattern of welfare services.

The Catholic church considers its social role as more immediately directed at shaping the social structure as well as the individual Christian life. In its relationship to the state in the field of social welfare the Catholic church regards government as an enabler to voluntary effort, basing its policies on the social philosophy principle of subsidiarity.

Although there are wide divergencies among them, the social action focus of many Jewish groups, unlike that of Protestants and Catholics, is directed towards a secular society. This presents a secular-religious conflict among the Jews and between Jews and Christians. The conflict is reflected in the dichotomy that separates religious from lay Jewish institutions, the social role of the Jewish community being carried largely by lay institutions, so that social action and social welfare programs tend to be removed from the control of the Jewish religious groups. To what extent this has resulted in a secularization of Jewish agencies is disputed by Jews.

4

A MATTER OF LAW

THE role conception that an institution has of itself is only one of the determinants of its social character; equally if not more important in determining social role is the role expectation of others. The social role that society assigns to the churches is to a considerable degree pictured in the law. The history of the law reflects a pattern of relationship between voluntary and government welfare and so indicates certain guidelines for determining the role of voluntary welfare in the welfare state. This chapter is an examination of the law governing this relationship. Because of the church-state problem involved in this relationship, our primary concern will be with government and sectarian welfare.

THE LAW AND WELFARE

For over a hundred years there has existed in the United States a partnership between local governments and sectarian welfare. In 1868, for example, when the question of state aid to sectarian institutions came before the Constitutional Convention of New York State, the Convention almost unanimously upheld the practice on the ground that it was "a mere matter of expediency and economy" to the state.[1] But the classic legal recognition for the practice of state aid to church-related welfare institutions was given by the U.S. Supreme Court in its decision on *Bradfield* v. *Roberts* [2] in 1899.

[1] *Grants of Land and Gifts of Money*, p. 20.   [2] 175 U.S. 299 (1899).

This case involved the legal right of the District of Columbia to hand over to Providence Hospital, conducted by the Sisters of Charity of the Catholic church, a $30,000 appropriation for the construction of two isolation wards for contagious disease cases. Also in question was the authorization of the Commissioners of the District to pay the hospital $250 a year for each patient treated therein. This enactment was challenged on the ground that tax money was being used to support a religious institution and that this was a violation of the First Amendment. The decision of the court distinguished a welfare institution qua secular institution fulfilling a public purpose from a welfare institution qua church institution. "The Court reasoned that the hospital was a separate legal entity with a secular purpose and that its ownership and management by Catholic sisters did not make it a religious organization." [3] Neither the belief of the individuals who incorporated the hospital nor the auspices under which it was incorporated was pertinent. The only pertinent factor was its legal incorporation. In the language of the Court:

Whether the individuals who compose the corporation under its charter happen to be all Roman Catholics, or all Methodists, or Presbyterians, or Unitarians, or members of any other religious organization, or of no organization at all, is not the slightest consequence with reference to the law of its incorporation.[4]

Even the fact that a corporation has a sectarian policy and is operated for certain defined purposes does not convert it into a religious or sectarian body or alter its legal character.

In effect then, the Court judged that a sectarian institution may enter into partnership with the state without violating the principle of church-state separation. The state enters into a contract with the institution as a civil entity, not as a religious body.[5] Therefore, the state may use sectarian institutions just as it may other legally incorporated institutions.

---

[3] Maximillian W. Kempner, "The Supreme Court and the Establishment and Free Exercise of Religion," in *Religion and the Free Society* (New York, The Fund for the Republic, 1958), p. 90.

[4] *Bradfield* v. *Roberts*, 175 U.S. 299 (1899).

[5] F. Ernest Johnson, ed., *Religion and Social Work*, p. 165.

A 1917 decision of the Supreme Court of Illinois on a similar case defined the church-state relationship more incisively. The court reasoned that if the county paid the institution somewhat less than the actual cost of care, this could hardly be called "aid" to a sectarian organization, and so would not be a violation of the Constitution.[6]

In the case of *Schade v. Allegheny County* [7] the Supreme Court of Pennsylvania gave a ruling similar to that of the Supreme Court of Illinois. Article III, Section 18, of the constitution of Pennsylvania provides that

No appropriation, except for pensions or gratuities for military services, shall be made for charitable, educational or benevolent purposes, to any person or community, nor to any denominational or sectarian institution, corporation or association.

By thus forbidding an appropriation to any sectarian institution, corporation, or association, the constitution would seem to render invalid in Pennsylvania an interpretation similar to that made by the Supreme Court in the District of Columbia. The plaintiffs in the Pennsylvania case alleged that Allegheny County was acting in violation of Article III by appropriating tax funds for the support, care, and maintenance of delinquent, neglected, or dependent children placed in sectarian homes and institutions by the county juvenile court. The plaintiffs contended further that the payments tended toward an "establishment of religion" and so were in violation of the Fourteenth Amendment.

The court based its decision on the ground that payments made for the support and maintenance of children under the jurisdiction and control of the juvenile court are not appropriations within the meaning of the term as used in Article III of the constitution. The court argued:

The cost of the maintenance of neglected children either by the State or the County is neither a charity nor a benevolence, but a governmental duty. All the plaintiffs proved was that the monies received by the defendant institutions were in *partial reimbursement* for the cost of room and board of such minors.

[6] Arlien Johnson, *Public Policy and Private Charities*, p. 80.
[7] 28 Pa. 185 (1956).

The Supreme Court of Pennsylvania then extended its interpretation of the state constitution beyond this particular case to a broader church-state relationship:

The Constitution does not prohibit the State or any of its agencies from doing business with denominational or sectarian institutions, nor from payng just debts to them when incurred at its direction or with its approval.

Then addressing itself to the charge that payments to denominational or sectarian institutions tend toward government "establishment of religion," the Pennsylvania Court summarily dismissed the matter by reference to a previous U.S. Supreme Court decision:

The Supreme Court has, in principle, settled it adversely to the appellant's position. See *Everson* v. *Board of Education* . . . where it was held that a State's use of public tax funds for the transportation of pupils to and from sectarian schools did not serve to promote the establishment of religion.

The passage in 1947 of Title VI of the Public Health Service Act has offered the most recent opportunities for testing the constitutionality of government support for sectarian institutions. Because of the heavy costs of constructing, equipping, and operating hospitals and because of the increasing demand for more hospitals throughout the United States, the Federal government sought to encourage the construction, replacement, and remodeling of hospitals and related medical facilities. Through this legislation, known as the Hill-Burton Hospital Construction Act, a varying percentage, depending upon the state, of the total cost of hospital construction is made available through Federal grants to state and local governments and to private sectarian and nonsectarian institutions. One condition of eligibility for Hill-Burton funds is nondiscrimination by reason of race, creed, or national origin. Federal tax funds therefore are available to sectarian hospitals. This enactment has, perhaps more than any other in our social welfare history, been responsible for denominational agencies' examination of their policies and attitudes toward the acceptance of government assistance.

The constitutionality of the Hill-Burton Act has been tested several times in the state courts. The 1949 Kentucky case, *Kentucky*

Building Commission v. *Effron*,[8] is typical. In 1948 the General
Assembly of Kentucky had created the Division of Medical Hospitals and Related Services in the Department of Health, the division
to serve as an instrument of the state for the administration of the
Hill-Burton Act. In the same year the Assembly had also appro-
priated $10 million to be used as matching funds for the construc-
tion of city, county, and nonprofit private hospitals. The purpose
of the state appropriation was additional encouragement for voluntary hospital construction in the state.

The plantiffs in the Kentucky case contested the constitutionality
of the appropriations for private sectarian organizations on the
ground that the state constitution forbids grants except in consideration of public service. After ruling that "the construction of nonprofit hospital facilities is a public purpose," the Kentucky Court of
Appeals distinguished between the auspices of an institution and its
purpose: "A private agency may be utilized as a pipe-line through
which a public expenditure is made, the test being not who receives
the money, but the character of the use for which it is expended."
In the closing statement of its decision the court reviewed the place
of private sectarian agencies vis-à-vis state and Federal governments:

> In their inception, hospitals were charitable organizations sponsored by
> religious sects which owned and operated them. In recent years the
> National and State Governments have enacted much social legislation in
> an endeavor to relieve charitable institutions in caring for the sick. . . .
> Recognizing that these institutions were in existence and being operated
> efficiently through their own boards, the Federal and State Governments
> have thought it more practical to aid them rather than to build new ones.
> Certainly, it was never the intention of the framers of Section 5 of our
> Constitution to prevent the State from aiding with monies raised by taxes
> an institution rendering a public service merely because the governing
> body of the institution is composed of one denomination.

WELFARE AND EDUCATION

Executives and policy-makers who consider the matter of church-
state policies in welfare always do so with an eye to policies of
church and state separation that prevail in education. One has only

[8] 220 S.W.2d. 836 (1949).

to study the discussions of church welfare executives to see how gingerly they formulate policies of church-state in welfare in order not to compromise policies of church-state in education. Church-state issues in welfare are not isolated from other policy issues; a church-state policy in one social context raises questions of policy in other contexts. For this reason policies of church-state separation in education enter into this present study.

Specifically, it seems that on the basis of social philosophy the church-state issue in social welfare should be grounded on the same principles as the church-state issue in education. Yet the tradition is otherwise. In practice, as in the courts, one principle has determined church-state separation in education; and quite another, divergent principle has determined church-state cooperation in welfare. In the face of these divergent principles, policy-makers in welfare differ in their recommendation. Some separationists would apply to welfare the principle that now obtains in education, separation of church and state. Some cooperationists would apply to education the principle that now obtains in welfare, cooperation of church and state. Others would distinguish the two areas, retaining in welfare the principle of cooperation and in education the principle of separation.

Although the legal tradition of the courts is to distinguish education from welfare services, certain cases have shown how slender the line of distinction can be. The New York state constitution prohibits the appropriation of tax money for denominational schools but allows appropriations for the needy and for child care even if the care is provided in sectarian institutions. In the case of *Sargent* v. *Board of Education* [9] in 1904, the plaintiff challenged the right of the state to appropriate money for St. Mary's Boys' Orphan Asylum of Rochester, a Catholic institution whose activities included an educational program. It was argued that the appropriation constituted aid to sectarian education. The court held that the objections of the plaintiff were unreasonable, since it was impracticable for the orphans to be educated outside the institution and that the education program did not change the child-welfare character of the institution. Therefore, Article IX, Section 4, of the

[9] 177 N.Y. 317, 69 N.E. 722 (1904).

constitution, which prohibits appropriations to sectarian schools, did
not apply in this case. The appropriation was rendered valid under
Article VIII, Section 14, which permits appropriations for welfare
purposes.

In New York City the expenditures of public monies for voluntary day-care centers were for years uncontested, even though
many of the centers were conducted by religious groups. But when
several centers were established on sectarian school premises, the
rights of these centers to public funds were challenged. The case of
Sargent v. *Board of Education* had involved a sectarian educational
program in an institution not essentially educational. The matter of
publicly supported day-care centers on parochial school premises
involved a welfare program in a sectarian educational institution.
In 1943 the Attorney General of the State of New York ruled that
the maintenance of a child-care project in an educational institution
under religious auspices was in violation of Article XI, Section 4,
of the state constitution even if the program was conducted outside
of school hours. The determining factor in the decision was, not
that the program was under religious auspices nor that it was conducted on property owned by a sectarian corporation but that the
program was conducted in a school building where the education
was based on the tenets of a religious denomination. Because of this
tie-in of a welfare with an education service, "the day care center
was held to be an indirect aid to the parochial school." [10]

This decision, however, was later reversed. After much study
and many conferences, the Attorney General ruled that the government's support of the noneducational facilities of denominational
schools could not be held to foster the educational functions of such
schools. Because of this reversed decision the State Youth Commission and the New York City Youth Board have been able to contract with sectarian welfare agencies for services to youth and their
families. These agencies in turn are able to use the much-needed
premises and facilities of sectarian educational institutions.

Then there are the two Supreme Court cases pertinent to the field
of education that developed the "child benefit theory." In the Lou-

[10] Guilfoyle, "Church-State Relations in Welfare," *Catholic Lawyer*, III, No.
2 (April, 1957), 125.

isiana textbook case the court upheld the right of the state to provide textbooks from tax funds for children attending sectarian schools on the grounds that not the church school but "the school children and the state alone are the beneficiaries." [11] In the New Jersey bus transportation case the court sustained the right of the local board of education to provide free transportation for children attending sectarian schools.[12] In allowing tax-paid books and services to sectarian school children, the court equivalently rules "that the state's obligation to all the children in the state transcends a too-literal observance of the principle of separation of church and state." [13] The "child benefit theory" raises the question in many minds as to what should be considered a benefit, and how far the state may go in granting benefits to sectarian school children.

WELFARE, EDUCATION, AND RELIGION

Church welfare leaders are aware how thin is the legal distinction separating church-state cooperation in welfare from church-state separation in education, and some fear that church-state welfare policy may edge its way into church-state educational policy. Hence, welfare policies are formed with one eye on church-state policies in education.

In its *Christian Social Action,* for example, the 169th General Assembly of the Presbyterian Church, U.S.A., introduced its policy statement on welfare with a statement not on welfare but on education: "We are unalterably opposed to the use of public funds for parochial schools." The statement continues: "We recognize that at the present time the old problem of relations between the church and the state is of increasing importance and reaches far beyond this matter of education." [14] Accordingly the Assembly approved the following policy, which had been adopted by the National Presbyterian Health and Welfare Association:

11 *Cochran* v. *Louisiana State Board of Education,* 281 U.S. 370, 50 Sup.Ct. 335 (1930).

12 *Everson* v. *Board of Education,* 330 U.S. 1, 67 Sup.Ct. 504 (1947).

13 Spurlock, *Education and the Supreme Court,* p. 76.

14 General Assembly of the Presbyterian Church, U.S.A., *Christian Social Action,* p. 9.

Presbyterian health and welfare work should utilize public sources of help for two purposes: the purchase of services in behalf of needy persons, and grants for capital expenses, provided again that such payments do not imperil church control, compromise basic principles, or interfere with their proclamation of the gospel.[15]

This policy was confirmed in May, 1959, by the 171st General Assembly in Indianapolis.[16]

The General Assembly is therefore "unalterably opposed" to the use of tax funds for sectarian education but affirms that Presbyterian agencies "should utilize" tax funds for sectarian welfare where this can be done without compromising basic principles. Pragmatic considerations seem to play a significant part in the policy affirmed by the Presbyterian Health and Welfare Association. At least, the executive secretary of the Association, implied this attitude when he stated that the only basic questions demanding answers are: "Who can do the job? Who will do the job? Who can pay for the job?"[17]

In the last analysis pragmatism is the determining factor: "Americans apply in actuality only one test—what works? As someone has remarked, 'We have always been wise enough not to be bound by any ideology.'"[18] The secretary pointed out that social welfare has brought church and state into cooperative relationships in mental hospitals, prisons, institutions, child-welfare services, and the armed forces. The secretary considers among other areas of church-state cooperation that of chaplaincy programs in welfare institutions:

This is an ideal example of pragmatic development: the churches train the chaplains and ordain them. Government puts them to work in hospitals, mental institutions, prisons, and correctional institutions for minors. Ideologically, this is all wrong and an apparent violation of the principle of the separation of church and state. Pragmatically, it works beautifully and the spiritual needs of patients and inmates are met.[19]

The Presbyterians are not alone in maintaining a separation policy

[15] National Presbyterian Health and Welfare Association, "Presbyterian Church and Welfare," p. 3.

[16] National Presbyterian Health and Welfare Association, "Report of Special Hospital Study Committee," p. 10.

[17] Lee, "State of Voluntarism in Social Welfare Today," p. 4.

[18] *Ibid.*   [19] *Ibid.*, p. 5.

in education and a cooperation policy in welfare. The executive secretary of the Department of Social Welfare of the Evangelical and Reformed Church wrote that his denomination traditionally accepts public funds for welfare programs. At the same time the church leaders are careful to continue "our rigid philosophy of the separation of Church and State." [20] Hill-Burton construction funds and funds for services to children and the aged are accepted, but church leaders "present these programs as health and welfare activities rather than as opportunities for Evangelism." [21]

In the course of further correspondence the executive secretary wrote: "There is a decided line of distinction between aid to direct welfare services and those involving education, and inevitably evangelism." [22] The distinction then on which this church seems to base the difference between its policies in education and its policies in welfare is that welfare institutions are not "opportunities for evangelism" but educational institutions are. This executive commented on his position this way: "While there are some who suggest that this is a fine line of distinction, we insist that the distinction is quite clear and that a careful analysis would eliminate any confusion on the part of one who considers it." [23]

A similar distinction is apparently upheld by the bishops of the Methodist church. At their annual meeting, in April, 1961, they maintained that anyone who seeks tax aid for private schools "confuses support for the social welfare of children with the provision for sectarian religious instruction." [24] The position is that sectarian welfare institutions are eligible for tax funds, since sectarian welfare agencies do not further sectarian ends, whereas sectarian educational institutions are ineligible for tax funds, since sectarian schools are "a furtherance of sectarian ends." [25]

But to other churchmen this is, as one Methodist theologian put it in an interview with the author, "speaking out of both sides of our mouth." In his opinion, however theoretically one might distinguish between educational and welfare functions, the problems

---

20 Letter to the author, March 17, 1961. 21 *Ibid.*
22 Letter to the author, April 27, 1961.
23 Letter to the author, March 17, 1961.
24 Boston *Globe*, April 7, 1961, p. 15. 25 *Ibid.*

involved make the distinction almost impossible in practice. He therefore opposes the acceptance of tax funds for sectarian welfare institutions and during the interview posed the problem that must face those who draw this line of distinction: Suppose you accept, he said, Hill-Burton funds for a hospital to which a nursing home is added. Are you going to accept funds for the nursing home, which contains classrooms in which classes are conducted? Are you not then accepting funds for education, sectarian education at that?

Others are equally unsatisfied with a policy which depends on the maintenance of a clear line of differentiation between educational and welfare functions. In a report from the New York East Conference of the Fourth Assembly of the Board of Social and Economic Relations of the Methodist Church, it is pointed out that if Protestant groups cannot do a better job of clarifying and justifying their "divergent policies on public aid to church programs in *welfare* and *education*," they will be faced with the task of demonstrating "why policies now being followed by Protestants in social welfare . . . should not apply in Catholic elementary and secondary schools!" [26] Dean Kelley, of the Methodist church, says,

If we cannot convince neutral and hostile legislators that the principles of one do not apply to the other, we will soon find purchase-of-services and construction-subsidy policies being given to parochial schools in the form of scholarship aid to pupils, etc.[27]

Kelley posed the same problem at the 1961 Conference on Social Welfare of the National Council of Churches: "How can you oppose aid to Catholic parochial schools when your colleges and hospitals have been taking Federal money for years?" [28]

Jewish civil rights and community relations organizations raise the same objections and show the same uneasiness as they look at the legal line dividing aid to welfare from aid to education. Philip Jacobson, program coordinator of the National Community Relations Advisory Council, poses the same problem in a statement: "Many who are quite vocal in their opposition to tax funds for sec-

[26] Methodist Church, *Research Consultation on the Church and State*, concluding report of the Fourth Assembly, p. 2.   [27] *Ibid.*
[28] Quoted in New York *Times*, October 25, 1961, p. 22.

tarian education are strangely silent on, perhaps even active in their support of, state aid for religiously sponsored welfare agencies." [29]

In Jacobson's opinion, there is only a "fiction of an essential difference between education and welfare in respect to state aid." [30] Education and welfare, at least in practice, are inseparable. According to Jacobson, the child institutionalized in a sectarian agency is clearly "conditioned by the religious atmosphere of his surroundings." [31] In fact, as Jacobson notes, the child in a welfare institution may be more "conditioned" than one in an educational institution:

Is there any doubt that this type of institutional care can have a far greater bearing on the child's future thought and conduct, and could be a much more potent force in turning him to a specific religious tradition, than a formal religious education? [32]

According to this view, welfare is assimilated to education. Because welfare institutions have educational overtones, they should not receive financial assistance from government agencies.

Some Catholics recognize at least an area in which there is considerable overlapping of education and welfare. In an article on aid to sectarian education the Rev. Virgil Blum, professor of political science at Marquette University, distinguishes between aid to a sectarian school and aid to the child, who may then exercise his right to attend either a public or a private school. Blum bases his argument on two recognized rights: freedom of choice in education and the right to share equally in welfare benefits. Government, he says, may not demand the surrender of one constitutional right as a condition for the exercise of another. Government cannot, therefore, demand that a child surrender freedom of choice in education as a condition for receiving welfare benefits equally with other children. "In the distribution of benefits government must be objectively indifferent to the religious beliefs of its citizens." [33] His summary:

[29] Jacobson, "Community Relations Implications," *Journal of Jewish Communal Services*, XXXVII, No. 1 (Fall, 1960), 114.
[30] *Ibid.*, p. 116.   [31] *Ibid.*   [32] *Ibid.*
[33] Virgil C. Blum, "Freedom of Choice in Schools," *Homiletic and Pastoral Review*, LVIII, No. 1 (October, 1957), 29.

Children . . . have liberties and rights under the Federal Constitution. One of these rights is freedom of choice in education. Children who exercise this choice may not be deprived of other constitutional rights *because* they have exercised this right. Among such constitutional rights is the right to share equally with other children in welfare benefits. *Education itself is one of these benefits.*[34]

The difference between Jacobson's position and that of Blum seems to come to this: Both Jacobson and Blum see in welfare overtones of education; but whereas Jacobson sees welfare benefits as accruing to the institution, Blum sees welfare benefits as accruing to the individual and the individual free to use those benefits freely in the area of education.

Jacobson considers the position that makes education a welfare benefit a "startling theory"[35] and fears this might be the wedge for aid to sectarian education. Therefore, at the National Conference of Jewish Communal Services he pleaded with the executives that they not attempt to distinguish welfare from education where church-state matters are concerned:

In all of our dealing with the public we must, as in a court of equity, appear with "clean hands." Even if it be true that there is no legal impediment to the acceptance of state funds for religiously sponsored welfare services, there is still a moral dilemma.[36]

Then he put to the Jewish conference substantially the same question that Kelley put to the National Council of Churches: "If we accept these funds for our welfare services, what right do we have to deny state funds for religious education?"[37]

CONCLUSIONS

The purpose of this study is not to analyze or distinguish the relative merits of aid to sectarian welfare and aid to sectarian education. Neither is its purpose to evaluate the merits of aid to the sectarian student as against aid to the sectarian welfare client. We have merely presented a brief history of the law governing voluntary and

[34] *Ibid.*, p. 28.
[35] Jacobson, "Community Relations Implications," *Journal of Jewish Communal Services*, XXXVII, No. 1 (Fall, 1960), 117.
[36] *Ibid.*, p. 118.   [37] *Ibid.*

government welfare relationships and some of the implications this history has for broader church-state policy. The main conclusions from these considerations are:

There is a long history of tax support for sectarian welfare that has been many times tested in the courts.

The legal line distinguishing aid to sectarian welfare from aid to sectarian education is historically solid.

There are, however, instances in which areas of aid to sectarian welfare and education overlap, and here the line of distinction tends to be thin.

Among churchmen, some maintain that a policy favoring tax support to sectarian welfare does not compromise the traditional policy to deny tax support to sectarian education. Others, however, think that a policy of tax support to sectarian welfare implies in practice, if not in principle, a policy of tax support to sectarian education.

One senses a fear on the part of some that as society becomes increasingly characterized by the principle of the welfare state it will be characterized by a pattern of church-state cooperation that is common to the welfare field rather than a pattern of church-state separation that is common to the field of education.

5

A MATTER OF MONEY

THE conception that religious leaders entertain of the social role of the church and the role expectation that society has for the church are largely based on ideological values of a theological and political nature. These values one would expect to see reflected in the social institutions of the churches. Aware, however, that local administrators have practical problems that tend to bend policies away from pure ideological values, one may raise questions like the following: Do the policies and practices of local agencies coincide with and reflect the role conception of the churches? Do sectarian welfare agencies receive financial assistance from government? What policies do they have governing their relationship with government agencies?

It appeared that little was known on a national scale about the actual practices of church-sponsored welfare agencies with respect to receipt of government funds. Many national executive secretaries were unaware of the policies and practices of their own local church affiliates. Several of the national secretaries approached by the author expressed both interest in and ignorance of the practices and policies that guide the relationships of local agencies with government welfare.[1]

[1] The cooperation that the author received from sectarian national executive secretaries may be understood from the interest evidenced in the remark of one of these executives, who said, "This is the kind of information we should have of our own agencies, but do not have." (Interview, March, 1961.)

Therefore, with the help of many welfare executives and national secretaries, sectarian and nonsectarian, a questionnaire was designed to get answers to the questions stated above. The author discussed this aspect of the study in interviews with the executive secretaries of the Department of Social Welfare of the National Council of the Churches of Christ in the U.S.A., the National Conference of Catholic Charities, the Council of Jewish Federations and Welfare Funds, numerous Protestant national and state welfare agencies, with several directors of Catholic Charities, and with several Jewish welfare and community leaders.

National sectarian executives endorsed the study and by personal letter recommended it to their local agency administrators. This endorsement and recommendation by national sectarian welfare leaders was largely responsible for cooperation by local leaders.

In all cases national executives provided the study with up-to-date directories of their health and welfare agencies in 20 states: Alabama, California, Colorado, Connecticut, Georgia, Indiana, Kentucky, Maryland, Michigan, Minnesota, Missouri, New York, Ohio, Oregon, Pennsylvania, Rhode Island, South Carolina, Texas, Washington, and Wisconsin. These states were chosen because the agencies in many of their large cities had cooperated with the United Community Funds and Councils of America in their total expenditure studies. This affiliation gave some degree of assurance that the agencies in these cities would have already available the type of financial information that we were seeking for this study. These states are not presented as a representative sample of all states. If a bias exists, it is in the direction of including states with well-organized welfare services, as evidenced by the existence of central planning and financing bodies affiliated with the United Community Funds and Councils of America. It was hoped that in the larger cities at least some of the information needed in this present study would be readily available from many of the local administrators.

Questionnaires were sent in these states to all the church-related hospitals, nursing homes for the aged, children's institutions, and children's services under the auspices of the American Baptist, Southern Baptist, Episcopal, Evangelical and Reformed, and Jewish denominations and to approximately 70 percent of the Methodist,

56 percent of the Lutheran, and 47 percent of the Catholic agencies.[2] Schedules were sent to a sampling of the nonsectarian agencies listed in the health and welfare directories of the following cities: Albany (New York), Atlanta, Baltimore, Birmingham, Buffalo, Cleveland, Columbus (Ohio), Dallas, Dayton, Denver, Detroit, Houston, Indianapolis, Kansas City, Louisville, Los Angeles, Milwaukee, New Haven, Philadelphia, Pittsburgh, Portland (Oregon), Providence, Rochester, Saint Louis, San Francisco, Seattle, Spartanburg (South Carolina), and Toledo.

It was undesirable to sample the agencies in the study by strict random sampling methods for two reasons. First, the number of welfare agencies varies greatly from denomination to denomination. American Baptists list 77 institutions throughout the country, Southern Baptists 81, and Methodists 244, while Catholics list thousands. Second, denominations tend to specialize in particular types of services. Most Protestant groups have a relatively larger number of homes for the aged and relatively fewer children's services. Methodists, for example, list 117 services for the aged against 49 for children. Catholics, by contrast, have 325 institutions for the aged and 450 for children. In order to assure a substantial number of responses, therefore, the Jewish and certain Protestant denominations were oversampled.

Of the agencies that were invited to participate in the study, the Jewish agencies were by far the most cooperative. This tendency might be explained in part by the fact that the study was conducted from Brandeis University, but the study was also presented to Protestant and Catholic agency administrators with the written endorsement and recommendation of their national executive secretaries. About two-thirds of the Jewish agencies returned the questionnaires, a proportion almost twice that returned by the Catholic agencies (see Table 1). Although a large number of diocesan directors of Catholic Charities participated in the study, Catholic administrators were in general uncooperative. Of the 66 diocesan directors who were asked to participate, 39, more than half, accepted; but of the

---

[2] This 47 percent is exclusive of Catholic hospitals. Because of the large number of Catholic hospitals, only a small percentage was included in the sample.

remaining 257 Catholic institutions invited to cooperate in the study, only 68, about one-fourth, accepted.

The author's original concern was that the Protestants would be least cooperative, since the study was conducted by a Catholic priest from a university founded under Jewish auspices; but this concern was not borne out, since the proportion of Protestants responding was about the same as the proportion of the entire group responding. Catholics were considerably less responsive to the study than were Protestants, even though the request to the Catholic agencies was over the signatures of the executive secretary of the National Conference of Catholic Charities and of the author. The Protestant response varied somewhat according to denomination. Lutherans and Methodists were the most cooperative; American Baptists were least cooperative.[3]

TABLE 1. *Response to Questionnaires, by Affiliation*

Response	Nonsectarian	Jewish	Catholic	Protestant	Total
Returned	85	63	107	152[a]	407
Not returned	128	34	216	208	586
Other[b]	10	4	29	49	92
Total	223[a]	101	352	409	1,085

[a] Includes 6 questionnaires sent under the assumption that the agencies were nonsectarian, but returned with the information that they were Protestant, although the specific denomination was not indicated.

[b] Questionnaires that could not be used in the study because the agencies no longer existed or because the information given was insufficient.

Of the 993 potential participants, therefore, 407, or 41 percent, responded. The remaining 59 percent neither returned the questionnaires nor sent letters of explanation. To follow up this 59 percent in order to establish conclusively the statistical validity of the sample was too formidable an undertaking for the resources available to this study, nor was it thought necessary in order to answer the questions basic to the study.*

[3] We shall see later that these evaluations of cooperation on the basis of initial response will have to be qualified. A high percentage of Protestant agencies that receive tax funds did not fulfill the initial expectation of cooperation because they did not submit to the study a fiscal statement of their programs.

* For a more detailed breakdown by denomination, see Appendix I.

All external evidence, however, indicates that the sample is a good one. The sample is geographically representative. The sampling is representative of agency size; on the basis of annual budgets, small, medium, and large agencies are included. Furthermore, from what is known of denominational policies at the top executive level, there is reason to believe that the sample is not systematically biased.

The high percentage of the Jewish return would seem to be representative of Jewish agencies and so a valuable source of data.

Although the Catholic return was low in proportion to the total, it is representative of Catholic policy and practice in that schedules were received from 39 diocesan directors, each appointed by the local bishop. Furthermore, the policy thinking revealed in the questionnaires and in some cases the actual expression of local directors reflect generally accepted Catholic social philosophy as presented in the previous chapter.

The Protestant return can be adjudged representative for several reasons. The range of local-agency policies reflects the range of Protestant attitudes expressed in the long line of Protestant welfare conferences and workshops. The sample mirrors the range of Protestant church organization—from the episcopal type of church structure to the congregational type—and thus reflects the variation in social policy determinations.

One further observation should be made concerning the participants in the study. A breakdown of the agencies by type of service shows that institutions and services for children participated to a considerably higher degree than did hospitals and homes for the aged.* This was anticipated; it was presumed that programs for children generally have closer financial relationships with government and hence are presumed more capable of participating responsibly in a study of this type.

AGENCY POLICIES

In the framework of this study a policy may be defined as a course of action by which an agency is guided in carrying out its program.

* For a detailed breakdown by type of service, see Appendix I.

It would seem that by this time voluntary agencies would have formulated policies for their relationships with government agencies. The long history of ever-increasing financial aid from government should, one would suppose, have made policy formulation a matter of course. Failing this, it would seem that a scrupulous care for church-state relationships would long ago have urged upon voluntary agencies the formulation of policies on the acceptance of funds. That some agencies have formulated policies is revealed in this study, but also revealed are large areas of no policy and uncertainty about policy. Of the voluntary health and welfare agencies about 53 percent state that they have no policy about accepting tax funds, about 41 percent have a policy of accepting funds, about 5 percent have a policy to refuse funds, and about 1 percent are uncertain of

TABLE 2. *Policies of Agencies Regarding Government Funds,*
by Affiliation

Policy	Nonsec-tarian	Jewish	Catholic	Protestant	Total
Policy of accepting funds	28	23	66	51	168
Policy of refusing funds	1	...	...	18	19
Uncertain of policy	1	...	...	4	5
No policy, and do not receive funds	21	20	9	34	84
No policy, but receive funds	34	20	32	45	131
Total	85	63	107	152	407

their policy (Table 2). The largest area of uncertainty is among the nonsectarian agencies, about 65 percent of which have no policy; the smallest area is among Catholic agencies, about 38 percent of which have no policy.

If this absence of policy is surprising, it may perhaps be more surprising that of the 215 agencies that state they have no policy, 131, or about 61 percent, say that they do receive tax funds and hence are committed to government assistance. Whether or not the agencies realize it, they have a policy. They have decided on a course of action even if they do not realize how they have arrived at it. A written policy determines action, but action also generates a policy. The significance of this will be different for different denominations. It may be less alarming to those Catholic theologians and social philosophers who see minor administrative and no moral problems about accepting tax funds. But, as we have seen, for some Protestant and for many Jewish leaders the use of government funds involves moral principles or is at least a matter of political principle. One would suppose that national executives balk at seeing local administrators engaged in practices that conflict with these principles. They may be rather uneasy about having social policy determined at the grass roots by administrators who are rather unconcerned about reconciling welfare programs and policies with denominational theology and civil rights issues.

AGENCY BUDGETS

This absence of explicit policies about financial assistance from government agencies has not deterred voluntary welfare agencies from receiving tax funds. Of these agencies 71 percent have contractual agreements whereby they receive government assistance, usually in the form of purchase of service. Catholic agencies are somewhat above the average for all voluntary agencies, 83 percent of them accepting tax funds; Protestants are somewhat below the average for all agencies, 64 percent of their agencies accepting tax funds. Among the Protestant denominations the Episcopalians and Lutherans have the largest percentage of agencies receiving tax support. Among Methodists there is apparently much divided thinking on the matter of government assistance; a proportionately large percentage of their hospitals, for example, have received Hill-Burton grants, but a relatively small percentage of their welfare agencies receive tax funds or sell services to government agencies. All in all this much is clear: Notwithstanding the attitudes and convictions of theologians and sectarian policy-makers, many of whom condemn money transactions between government and sectarian agencies, at least some of the agencies of all denominations are engaged in these transactions.

There are several reasons why voluntary agencies that receive government funds are reluctant or unwilling to discuss their fiscal programs. First, they are anxious to retain the public's financial interest and approval. If the budget is large, people may decide the agency has sufficient funds and curtail their contributions; if the budget is small, people may decide that the agency is second-rate. Second, voluntary agencies are either reluctant or unwilling to admit either to themselves or to others how dependent they are on government assistance. Third, there is in our culture concern for the separation of church and state and hence a sense of guilt about sectarian group's receiving tax money under any circumstances and for any reason. If to these reasons are added the uncertainties and indecisions of many agencies about explicit policy and the strong positions that some theologians and civil-rights leaders have taken on sectarian agencies' accepting tax funds of any kind, it is understandable why many voluntary agencies are reluctant or unwilling to disclose their budgets.

Of the 290 agencies receiving tax funds, 227, or 78 percent, submitted to the author a budget statement.* The other 63, or 22 percent, either refused to speak of their fiscal affairs or gave so incomplete a picture that it was of no use to this study (Table 3).

TABLE 3. *Agencies Receiving Tax Funds and Willingness to Submit Financial Statement, by Affiliation*

Policy	Nonsectarian	Jewish	Catholic	Protestant	Total
Receive tax funds:					
Complete financial statement	47	39	73	68	227
Incomplete or no statement	15	2	16	30	63
Do not receive funds	23	22	18	54	117
Total	85	63	107	152	407

Just as the Jewish agencies were most cooperative in entering the study, so they were the most cooperative in submitting fiscal information.†

It was expected that many agencies would hesitate to disclose financial information. One national secretary whose agencies finally did participate in the study hesitated to seek the cooperation of the

---

* For a breakdown by denominational affiliation of agencies that receive tax support and their willingness to disclose their agencies' budgets, see Appendix II.
† For a picture of the size of the welfare agencies in this study, see Appendix III.

local administrators of his denomination's agencies. He was of the opinion that the study scrutinized too closely matters of church and state, and he was especially concerned about the similarity of church-state problems in education and welfare. Before he would enlist the cooperation of his denomination's agencies in this welfare study, he requested from the author the following certification:

that it is not the intent of your study, either by yourself or by any other person associated with you in the Roman Catholic Church, to utilize this material as a springboard in indicating that Protestants are now, in fact, utilizing government funds and that therefore an inclusion of legislation for parochial schools would be a normal extension of the present experience.[4]

This statement of conditions is an admission of the tensions and fears that confront welfare executives in this area of social welfare policy; it also suggests a reason why 22 percent of the agencies did not submit financial statements of their relationship with government. In this instance the requested certification was given; the national executive secretary submitted it to the local welfare administrators of his denomination, and they cooperated in this study.

REIMBURSEMENT FOR SERVICES

The question of primary importance in the matter of a voluntary agency's fiscal policy is: What percentage of the total budgets of these agencies is accounted for by tax funds? The 227 agencies that presented financial statements give a fairly good picture of the dependence of voluntary agencies on income from tax sources.

Figure 1 shows that most agencies receive a small percentage of total annual expenditures from tax sources; but some agencies receive from tax funds something more than 70 percent of their budgets, and a few receive more than 80 percent. In one nonsectarian agency all the cases handled are referred by government agencies; this voluntary agency receives from government 100 per-

[4] Letter from the national Executive Secretary of the Department of Welfare of a Protestant denomination, April 27, 1961.

cent reimbursement, and hence its operating budget is made up entirely of tax funds.*

Figure 1 also gives a picture of the percentage of agency budget that is supplied by tax funds, by agency affiliation.† Jewish agencies receive a relatively small percentage of their budgets from tax

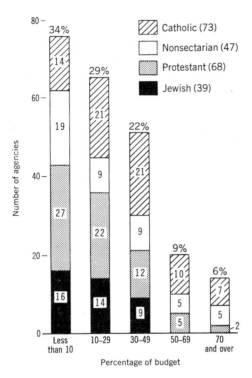

FIGURE 1. *Percentage of agency budget supplied from tax funds to 227 agencies, by affiliation.*

sources: of the 39 Jewish agencies in the sample, 17 receive less than 10 percent; none receive as much as 50 percent of annual budget.

* For a breakdown of these percentages by type of service—hospitals, homes for aged, children's institutions, children's services—see Appendix III.
† For a comparative picture of the amounts received per case per month by the four welfare categories in this study, see Appendix III.

Protestant agencies receive slightly higher percentages. Of the 68 Protestant agencies, 27 receive from tax funds less than 10 percent of annual budget, but 7 receive from government 50 percent or more of total budget. The nonsectarian and Catholic agencies receive a considerably larger proportion of total income from tax funds than do Protestant and Jewish agencies. Of the 49 nonsectarian agencies, 10 receive 50 percent or more of budget from government funds; of the 73 Catholic agencies 17 receive 50 percent or more of their budget from tax sources. Therefore, Jewish agencies seem to be most independent of tax funds and Catholic agencies most dependent upon tax funds.

What accounts for the variance in dependence on government assistance of the three sectarian groups? A partial explanation may be found in the variations in types of services represented in the sample.* As Table 4 shows, children's institutions, which receive the largest sums from government funds, are represented in only 6 of the 39 Jewish agencies, as compared with 28 of the 70 Protestant and 32 of the 71 Catholic. This may explain the lesser dependence of Jewish agencies on government funds, but it does not explain the greater dependence of Catholic agencies as against the lesser

TABLE 4. *Voluntary Agencies Receiving Tax Funds,
by Types of Service and Affiliation*

Type of Service	Jewish	Protestant	Nonsectarian	Catholic
Children's institutions	6	28	20	32
Homes for the aged	12	15	4	7
Children's services	13	10	11	26
Hospitals	8	17	12	6
Total	39	70	47	71

dependence of Protestant agencies. One reason for the difference between Catholic and Protestant dependence on government may be found in policy. The acceptance of government funds is compatible with Catholic welfare policy, but many Protestant agencies are undecided about the acceptance of government funds and hence approach government contracts with caution.

* For a complete presentation of variations in types of services, see Appendix III.

HILL-BURTON GRANTS

Reference has already been made to the Hill-Burton Hospital Construction Act. This piece of legislation has made grants for construction available to private hospitals, a considerable number of which are sectarian. Sectarian hospitals have traditionally carried a large share of the hospital burden of the nation; federal grants under the Hill-Burton Act have lightened that burden.

The first problem that one faces in research in this area is the difficulty in determining just what constitutes a sectarian hospital. Some hospitals of sectarian origin no longer claim a church affiliation. Because of this problem in arriving at a completely accurate count of a church's hospitals, it is difficult if not impossible to learn the exact total amount of funds received by a denomination under the Hill-Burton Act. The Catholic Hospital Association directory lists 889 hospitals,[5] the Protestant directories consulted yielded a total of 662 hospitals,[6] and the Jewish directory lists 57 hospitals.[7] These figures are exclusive of nursing homes.[8]

[5] *Hospital Progress*, Official Journal of the Catholic Hospital Association, Part II, Directory Issue (February, 1961), pp. 65–106.

[6] The basic Protestant directory is the *Directory of Protestant Hospitals and Institutions* (Chicago, American Protestant Hospital Association, January, 1960). For purposes of establishing denominational affiliations, the following directories were used:

American Baptists: *Concern*, VII, No. 1 (September–October, 1960), 14–16. (Multilith.)

Southern Baptists: *The Quarterly Review*, XXI, No. 3 (1961), 50.

United Church of Christ: *A Ministry of Hope*, Directory of Health and Welfare Institutions of the Evangelical and Reformed Church (St. Louis, The Commission on Benevolent Institutions).

Lutheran: *1960 Lutheran Health and Welfare Annual* (New York, National Lutheran Social Welfare Conference, 1960), pp. 69–100.

Methodist: *1961 Hospitals and Homes of the Methodist Church* (Chicago, Board of Hospitals and Homes of the Methodist Church, 1961). (Multilith.)

[7] *1958–59 Directory—Jewish Health and Welfare Agencies* (New York, Council of Jewish Federations and Welfare Funds). (Mimeographed.)

[8] Hill-Burton funds are also available for certain types of nursing homes but because of the difficulty in determining the eligibility of a nursing home for Hill-Burton grants from its description in a directory, all nursing homes have been intentionally excluded from this comparative study. Research grants are also available under the Hill-Burton Act, but these grants have likewise been excluded from this study.

One of the major problems was to determine what constitutes a Protestant hospital and its denominational affiliation. Some Protestant hospitals bear the names of specific denominations but are not listed in denominational directories. Such hospitals are, however, listed in the *Directory of Protestant Hospitals and Institutions* as being affiliated with the denominations whose names they bear. For our purposes here such hospitals are considered to be Protestant, but no attempt is made to presume to the specific affiliation. For this study Protestant hospitals are recognized as being of a specific denomination only if they are listed in a directory of that denomination.[9]

Therefore, according to the only sources that seem to be available, there are 1,608 sectarian hospitals, that is, hospitals recognized as affiliates of some denomination. There are, of course, differences

TABLE 5. *Number and Percentage of Sectarian Hospitals Receiving Hill-Burton Funds, by Affiliation*

Denomination	Number of Hospitals	Hospitals Receiving Funds	
		Number	Percent
Jewish	57	28	49
Catholic	889	370	41
Protestant:	662	236	35
Lutheran	116	71	61
Episcopal	49	19	38
Methodist	76	46	60
American Baptist	7	2	...
Southern Baptist	40	12	30
Evangelical and Reformed	9	5	...
Other	365	81	22
Total	1,608	634	39

in the number of hospitals under the administration of each denomination; there are differences in amounts received, and there are marked differences in the number of Protestant, Catholic, and Jewish hospitals that have received Hill-Burton grants (Table 5).*

[9] The only exception is the Episcopal hospitals, for which no special directory is available. Hospitals designated as Episcopal in this study are those so listed in the *Directory of Protestant Hospitals and Institutions*.

* For a complete picture of the Hill-Burton grants to sectarian hospitals and a comparison of amounts received by the different denominations, see Appendix IV.

Percentagewise, Lutheran hospitals outrank the hospitals of the other denominations, 71 out of 116, or 61 percent, receiving Hill-Burton funds. Among 889 Catholic hospitals, 370, or 41 percent, received grants.[10]

Figure 2 is a summary comparison of the number of sectarian hospitals, the number receiving Hill-Burton grants, and the amounts

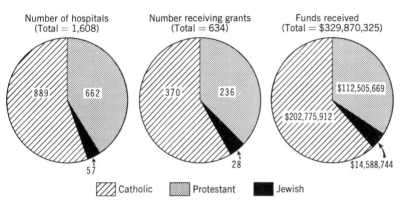

Number of hospitals (Total = 1,608)

Number receiving grants (Total = 634)

Funds received (Total = $329,870,325)

889   662   57

370   236   28

$112,505,669 $202,775,912 $14,588,744

▨ Catholic   ▦ Protestant   ■ Jewish

FIGURE 2. Sectarian hospitals receiving Hill-Burton grants compared by affiliation, number, and amount.

received. Protestants provide 41.2 percent of the nation's sectarian hospitals; of the sectarian hospitals receiving grants, 37.2 percent are Protestant; and of the total amount of Hill-Burton funds granted to sectarian hospitals, 34.1 percent have gone to Protestant hospitals. The disproportion is obvious: although Protestants provide 41.2 percent of the sectarian hospitals, only 37.2 percent of these hospitals receive grants. Protestant hospitals, therefore, are 4 percentage points below their expected participation in grants. Presuming equal eligibility of Protestant hospitals for Hill-Burton grants, it may be

[10] U.S. Department of Health, Education and Welfare, *Hospital and Medical Facilities Project Register—December 31, 1960* (Washington, D.C., U.S. Department of Health, Education and Welfare, Public Health Service, Division of Hospital and Medical Facilities, 1961). This *Register* gives a complete listing of all projects approved under Title VI of the Public Health Service Act. The Division of Hospital and Medical Facilities does not keep a record of the denominational affiliations of hospitals to which grants are made. The statistics in the present study were obtained by checking the *Register* against the denominational hospital directories enumerated in notes 5–7 above.

conjectured that this disproportion is explained by reluctance on the part of some Protestant administrators to accept government funds for reasons of church-state separation.

Catholics provide 55.3 percent of the nation's sectarian hospitals; of the sectarian hospitals receiving grants, 58.4 percent are Catholic; of the total amount of Hill-Burton funds granted to sectarian hospitals, 61.5 percent have been given to Catholic hospitals. Here the disproportion is the reverse of the Protestant: although Catholics provide only 55 percent of the nation's sectarian hospitals, 58 percent of these hospitals receive grants, and thus Catholic hospitals are 3 percentage points above their expected participation in Hill-Burton grants. This difference can be accounted for by the readiness of Catholic hospital administrators to accept government funds, which in this case were made available presumably by the reluctance of some Protestant hospitals to accept them.

Jews supply 3.5 percent of the nation's sectarian hospitals; 4.4 percent of the sectarian hospitals receiving grants are Jewish; of the total amount of Hill-Burton funds granted to sectarian hospitals, 4.4 percent have gone to Jewish hospitals. Although Jews provide only 3.5 percent of the sectarian hospitals, 4.4 percent of their hospitals receive grants. Jewish hospitals, therefore, are slightly above their expected participation in Hill-Burton funds; and again it may be presumed that this difference is made available by the Protestant reluctance on issues of church-state separation.

Two factors apparently account for the fact that Catholic hospitals receive more per institution than Protestant hospitals. The first is the relatively large number of Lutheran hospitals receiving grants and the small average of the amounts of the grants, coupled with the general tendency of the Lutheran hospitals to be concentrated in the relatively rural Middle West and Northwest. The second is the geographical distribution of Protestant and Catholic hospitals. The high concentration of Catholic hospitals is in the urban areas of New England, the East Coast, and the Northeast. The high concentration of Protestant hospitals is in the South Atlantic states and in the rural regions of the Northwest and the Rocky Mountains (Table 6).

Of all Catholic hospitals receiving Hill-Burton grants, 155, or

41.9 percent, are located in the urban regions of New England, the East Coast, and the Northeast as compared with only 54, or 22.8 percent, of Protestant Hill-Burton hospitals in the same areas. On the other hand, of all Protestant Hill-Burton hospitals, 126, or 53.4 percent, are located in the rural regions of the South Atlantic,

TABLE 6. Comparison of Protestant and Catholic Hospitals Receiving Hill-Burton Grants in Urban and Rural Areas

Area	Protestant	Catholic	Total
Urban[a]	54	155	209
Rural[b]	126	121	247
Total	180	276	456

[a] New England, East Coast, Northeast.
[b] South Atlantic, Northwest, Rocky Mountain.

the Northwest, and the Rocky Mountains as compared with only 121, or 32.7 percent, of the Catholic hospitals. The Rocky Mountain area is the only region where the number of Protestant Hill-Burton hospitals exceeds that of the Catholic.*

The average larger grant to the Catholic as compared with the Protestant hospitals would seem to be accounted for by the fact that grants in the urban areas, where Catholic hospitals are predominant, would generally be to larger institutions, while grants in the rural areas, where Protestant hospitals are predominant, would generally be to smaller institutions.

CONCLUSIONS

From the foregoing data on the policies and practices of sectarian agencies receiving tax funds, the following conclusions may be made:

Most voluntary agencies have not formulated policies about accepting or rejecting tax funds.

Where policies have been established they are almost always to accept tax support, rarely to reject it.

A large number, 61 percent, of the agencies that say they have

* For a detailed geographical presentation of the Protestant and Catholic Hill-Burton hospitals, see Appendix IV.

no policies about tax support are receiving tax support. Actually they have very significant policies without realizing it.

An extremely large number of agencies, 71 percent, have contractual agreements with government agencies whereby they receive tax funds, usually by way of selling services to government. At least some of the agencies of all denominations are engaged in these transactions.

Generally the tax support an agency receives is a small percentage of its total budget, but there are some agencies that receive well over 50 percent of their budget as a result of government contracts. Jewish agencies tend to receive a smaller percentage, Catholic agencies a larger percentage of their budgets from tax funds.

Although the Hill-Burton Act has been condemned by some religious groups as unconstitutional, a large number of hospitals of all denominations have received substantial grants for hospital construction under the act. Protestant, Catholic, and Jewish hospitals are apparently receiving a proportionately nearly equal share in the benefits of the act.

The policies and practices of some denominations are in conflict with the conception that religious leaders have of the social role of the church and the relationship they would like to see sectarian agencies maintain with the state. Not only are many sectarian agencies accepting tax funds through contractual agreements not based on a thought-out policy, but frequently also their practices are in spite of the policy indecision of higher executives, and sometimes even contrary to their policy decisions.

6

POLICY IN THE MAKING

ALTHOUGH most agency administrators lack formal policies relating their agencies to government, they are involved in definite agency practices that are not in line with church policies and may even conflict with them. These practices, it may be assumed, are based on certain attitudes of the local administrators or their boards. Two crucial issues affecting voluntary agency policy and practice in its relationships to government are: What threats to agency autonomy does the local agency administrator see in contracts to receive government funds? Does the attitude of the agency administrator reflect a philosophy of church-state separation or a philosophy of cooperation? [1]

To learn the attitudes of sectarian welfare agencies toward church-state relationships with respect to government support, a series of questions * was presented to agency administrators. The purpose was to arrive at some understanding of the confusion or dichotomy in welfare policy and practice—why many agencies are undecided about policy, while other agencies whose denominational representatives oppose government assistance are already involved in programs that include government assistance—and to determine whether local welfare agencies reflect a trend to a revision of policy on church-state relationships. In substance, the questions presented to

[1] References in the notes to agency administrators' responses will hereinafter give denomination, type of agency, and state where located.
* See Appendix V.

administrators were: Do local administrators favor or reject subsidy as sound policy? What distinction, if any, do they make between subsidy and purchase of service? Are there ideological objections which are responsible for indecision in determining policy?

SUBSIDY OF VOLUNTARY SERVICES

Both Protestant and Catholic national welfare executives generally agree that government subsidy of voluntary agencies involves risk; but among local agencies, even agencies within a denomination, there is disagreement.

Separation of Church and State

Underlying this disagreement there is first the issue of church and state. A total of 252 local administrators presented their views on the degree of compatibility of administrators' church-state principles with the acceptance of government subsidy. Catholics and Jews in welfare see the acceptance of subsidy as infringing only slightly on their principles of church and state. Of 58 Catholic agencies, 54 see no real conflict over church-state separation and government subsidy; of 45 Jewish agencies, 38 see no real conflict. No Catholics and only two Jews regard acceptance of subsidy as an extreme violation of the church-state principles, but there is less agreement among Protestant and nonsectarian administrators. Of 51 nonsectarian agencies, almost one-half see considerable or extreme church-state conflict over accepting subsidy; of 98 Protestant agencies, 58 see the same degree of conflict.

Agency Autonomy

The second issue underlying disagreement on government subsidy is the threat that subsidy presents to an agency's autonomy. In general, there is no agreement among administrators as to what effect subsidy has or is likely to have on an agency's program. Slightly more than half seem to think that subsidy is not harmful to their agencies; slightly less than half think it is harmful. Of the four groups in the study, the Jewish agencies have the least fear of the effects of subsidy on their agencies.

The significance of agencies' attitudes on the issues of church-state separation and autonomy is seen only when these two attitudes are examined together. In the matter of subsidy versus church-state infringement, more administrators see no problem than in the matter of subsidy versus agency autonomy. Protestant, Jewish, and nonsectarian administrators indicate relatively little difference in attitude on these two issues, but Catholic administrators indicate considerable difference in attitude. As Table 7 shows, most Catholics

TABLE 7. Agency Attitudes toward Subsidy and Church-State Separation, as Compared with Attitudes toward Subsidy and Agency Autonomy, by Affiliation

Denomination	Church-State Separation		Agency Autonomy	
	Total Number of Agencies	Subsidy Severe Violation, Percent	Total Number of Agencies	Subsidy Severe Threat, Percent
Protestant	98	59	104	65
Nonsectarian	51	43	52	40
Jewish	45	16	45	16
Catholic	58	7	63	37
Total	252	36	264	45

are not concerned about subsidy as a violation of church-state separation, but a considerable number of them see subsidy as threatening the autonomy of their agencies. Protestant, Jewish, and nonsectarian administrators tend to see both questions under more or less the same light. A small proportion of Protestants see subsidy as a church-state violation, and more or less the same percentage also see subsidy as a danger to the agency. About one-half of the administrators of Jewish agencies consider subsidy no church-state violation, and almost that same proportion also regard subsidy as a policy that will not endanger the voluntary agency. By contrast, few Catholics see subsidy as violating a church-state principle, but many see it as a possible threat to their autonomy.* Here again Catholic and Jewish agencies tend to see a greater compatibility be-

* For a detailed breakdown by denomination of the attitudes of agency administrators towards subsidy and the church-state principle as compared with their attitudes towards subsidy and agency autonomy, see Appendix V.

tween subsidy and agency control than do Protestant and non-sectarian agencies. Catholic administrators express considerably stronger concern than do Jews over loss of agency autonomy.

PURCHASE OF VOLUNTARY SERVICES

In the early 1930s Arlien Johnson made a clear distinction between subsidy of a voluntary agency and purchase of service. Recently, however, she has expressed the opinion that purchase of service, if continued over a long period of time, is only another form of subsidy. Speaking of her 1930 views, she said in retrospect:

I wrote hopefully that the practices which were emerging—purchase of service—"promise to relieve the public authorities of the hazards inherent in traditional, haphazard use of subsidies; but the success of the new arrangements would depend upon the further development of the science of public administration." [2]

Experience, she said, has proved that this hope has failed, "that there is a continuum between subsidy and purchase of service," that they differ only in degree. Hence, in 1959 she redefined subsidy in such a way that it included the continuing practice of purchasing service:

Any payment of a predetermined amount, made to a voluntary organization from public funds, in aid of or in compensation for care for a category of individuals served, where the payment is to be continued for a more or less indeterminate period of time and where the purpose is to provide care on an individual basis.[3]

Others clearly distinguish the two practices and so reject this continuum theory. Martha Branscombe rejects the soundness of subsidy as a policy and accepts the principle that public funds should be spent by public agencies as well as the correlative principle that private agencies should be voluntarily supported. Nevertheless, she

[2] Arlien Johnson, "Use of Public Funds by Voluntary Agencies," p. 19.
[3] *Ibid.* Miss Johnson refers to Werner's study of the pattern of subsidy and purchase of service that exists in all the states, which seems to indicate the continuum to which Miss Johnson refers. See Werner, *Public Financing.*

does not think that either of these principles precludes long-con-tinuing purchase of service.[4]

Katherine Lenroot, former chief of the Children's Bureau, ap-parently held the same distinction when she proposed the following administrative policy:

Public funds should be administered through public agencies, which, however, may utilize the services of private agencies when appropriate to meet the particular needs of individual children for whom the public agency has responsibility.[5]

In general, national executives also make a decided distinction between subsidy and purchase of service. As for local agency ad-ministrators, even if, as we have seen, they are divided on the sound-ness of subsidy, as we shall now see, they are not divided on the soundness of purchase of service as good policy, whether the con-sideration be church-state separation or agency autonomy.

Church-State Separation

Of the 349 local administrators who addressed themselves to the question of the degree of compatibility between their church-state principle and purchase of service, 89 percent see purchase of service as no violation at all or no significant violation of church-state sepa-ration. All Catholics favor purchase of service. Jews are not far below Catholics in unanimity, nearly all favoring purchase of service.

Opposing responses are to be found notably among nonsectarian and Protestant administrators, with most of the nonsectarian and Protestant administrators being in accord with Catholics and Jews, but with several nonsectarian and Protestant administrators regard-ing purchase of service as either a considerable or extreme violation of church-state separation. The ideological differences among the churches are perhaps best realized by comparing the 40 percent of Protestant executives with the 1 percent of Catholics who have some

[4] Branscombe, "Basic Policies and Principles of Public Child Care Services," *Child Welfare*, February, 1952 (special issue), p. 7.

[5] Katherine Lenroot, statement before the Senate Committee on Finance Hearings on H.R. 6000, January 20, 1950.

reservation about the validity of purchase of service in the light of the church-state principle.*

As we have seen, those denominations that are referred to as the "free church" tend to adhere to a much more conservative position on church-state separation. This conservatism is reflected in the attitudes of some Protestant administrators even toward purchase of service. Some Protestant agencies regard even purchase of service as an extreme violation of their church-state principles.

A brief historical digression will not be out of place in order to recall that there are well-rooted historical reasons for present Baptist and Methodist policies of church-state separation. The Calvinistic states of North America far from recognized full freedom of religion, which obtained only in Baptist Rhode Island and later in Pennsylvania, founded by the Society of Friends. Baptists and Methodists were in vigorous rebellion against the established Protestant churches. In the opinion of Troeltsch, "the parent of the 'rights of man' was therefore not actual Church Protestantism, but the Sectarianism and Spiritualism which it hated and drove forth into the New World." [6] The real foundations of the movement were laid in the English Puritan revolution and later extended to America, where this "step-child of the Reformation" had its "great hour in the history of the world." [7] These were the beginnings of the rigorous Baptist vigilance against even the slightest intimations of church-state cooperation, for a policy of cooperation may be construed to be or may actually transform itself into a wedge of establishmentarianism.

Among many groups this rigorous resistance to church-state cooperation still exists; among others it has been modified. The range of resistance among the denominations is delineated by the comments of local welfare administrators. These attitudes, some of them already crystallized in established policy, fall along a continuum from complete rejection of church-state cooperation in welfare to

---

* For a detailed breakdown by denomination of the attitudes of agency administrators towards purchase of service and the church-state principle as compared with their attitudes towards purchase of service and agency autonomy, see Appendix V.

[6] Troeltsch, *Protestantism and Progress*, p. 122.   [7] *Ibid.*, p. 124.

a solicitation of maximum cooperation. Before we sample this continuum, it is important to note that although some denominations are characterized by certain policies, no one denomination has one policy that is binding on all the agencies of that denomination. We must therefore expect to find contradictory attitudes within a denomination.

Absolute separatism, for example, is generally reflected in the attitudes of the Southern Baptist executives, as in these words of a Texas administrator: "Under no case should a church institution receive financial assistance from tax money." [8] Another classified both subsidy and purchase of service as extreme violations of church-state separation because "Baptists believe in the complete separation of church and State." [9] Another said that he had an established policy by which the agency had already rejected government funds of all types. He gave his reason for the policy:

Such a policy (to accept governmental funds) could allow any one group to monopolize the tax dollar. . . . Thus through the tax *all* are compelled to support a religion or cult to which many do not subscribe, and in which they have no voice. It becomes "taxation without representation." [10]

Many Southern Baptist administrators are aware of their church tradition and point to it as an influential factor in their policies: "The historic position of the Baptist churches within the Southern Baptist Convention has been and continues to be against any governmental subsidy for any of its churches or agencies supported by the churches." [11] Another expressed that historical tradition in a personal way: "I am a Baptist; I've lived and worked a long time with this policy of separation; I feel that it is right." [12]

But even among the Southern Baptists this historic position is here and there showing signs of weakening. One agency director indicated that a change in policy was in the offing: "We have been instructed not to accept any Hill-Burton type funds for any purposes until a committee of our denomination could fully make a

[8] Southern Baptist children's home, Texas.
[9] Southern Baptist hospital, Texas.
[10] Southern Baptist home for the aged, Missouri.
[11] Southern Baptist children's home, South Carolina.
[12] Southern Baptist children's home, Kentucky.

study regarding them." [13] The Baptist Hospital in Pensacola, Florida, did not wait for the matter to be studied but committed what the American Institute of Management called a "denominational heresy" by accepting a Hill-Burton grant of $780,000.[14]

One Missouri administrator whose hospital was receiving tax funds but who refused to state either the amount or the purpose for which the funds were received posed the plight in which his denomination's agencies find themselves. In a society where tax funds are becoming increasingly available, operational costs are continually rising, and standardization in accordance with new equipment and procedures involves heavy expenditure, there is pressure to accommodate principle to accepted social policy. As he expressed it: "We are opposed in principle, but recognize we must live under the laws of the land." [15] Theorists of social change frequently point to the social impact that religion and the church have on public policy and social structure. From this Southern Baptist example it is obvious that the reverse is also true: church policy and structure are significantly affected by and adapt themselves to the policies and structure of society.

Although American Baptists tend to identify in such matters with the Southern Baptists, they have less agreement as to what constitutes church-state violations in welfare. Some make a clear distinction between subsidy and purchase of service. One stated the rationale for the distinction: "I do not see any more conflict in taking payments for service rendered from a public agency than I do in complying with State requirements to operate the agency. The tie is inescapable." [16]

Two Evangelical and Reformed administrators, one from Missouri and one from Texas, expressed diametrically opposed policies on church-state separation in welfare, reflecting their denomination's present policy indecision and state of transition. The Missouri administrator considered both subsidy by and sale of service to

[13] Southern Baptist hospital, Texas.
[14] Villaume, "Church-State Relations in Social Welfare," p. 10.
[15] Southern Baptist hospital, Missouri.
[16] American Baptist children's home, Michigan.

government extreme violations of church-state separation. His reason was that "The church should not be a financial functionary of the Government in any way."[17] The Texas administrator said that, although his agency did not receive tax funds, it would accept both subsidy and purchase of service funds if the opportunity were offered. His reason was that "Separation of church and state is not involved so long as the agency serves a public need and offers its service to all people."[18]

Most Protestant agency directors distinguish subsidy from purchase of service, however, and see either no church-state violation or no violation of moment in purchase of service when carried out on a case-by-case basis. One Methodist administrator said: "As long as tax funds are made available for care of patients on the basis of purchase of service on an equitable cost basis, I can see no violation of the philosophy of separation of Church and State."[19] A Lutheran director made a similar distinction between subsidy and purchase of service:

As long as payments are made on a per case basis for the purchase of care, the degree of violation, if any, is minimal. In effect, the church agency becomes a contractor to government. To deny this possibility is practically to say state and church should never do business with each other.[20]

As a group, Lutheran administrators tend to reflect, more than do administrators of most other Protestant denominations, the thinking of their national executives. The following statement expresses the social philosophy of several Lutheran welfare conferences: "The provision of health facilities is a government problem and responsibility but best done in partnership with local and private agencies."[21]

Many Episcopal policies follow a similar line. One New York administrator wrote: "I can see no conflict if the criteria for public expenditures are based upon individual client need rather than sub-

[17] Evangelical and Reformed home for the aged, Missouri.
[18] Evangelical and Reformed home for the aged, Texas.
[19] Methodist hospital, Texas.   [20] Lutheran children's services, Wisconsin.
[21] Lutheran hospital, Missouri.

sidy of a sectarian program." [22] An Episcopal administrator in Ohio said that welfare service is social service whether given by a church-related agency or by any other: "We see no difference in paying a sectarian agency for care of dependent children than in payment to any other agency, if the same care is provided." [23]

The administrators are overwhelmingly positive in seeing no conflict between purchase of service and church-state separation. Catholic and Jewish agencies especially have no problem in accepting purchase of service, but there is considerable or extreme concern from a few of the Protestant agencies.*

Agency Autonomy

The question of church and state is ideological; the question of purchase of service and its effect on policy is practical and immediate. Local administrators are much more concerned about the effect of government contracts on their agencies' autonomy than they are about the effect of such contracts on the principle of church-state separation. It seems that the social change which the churches have had to face has made bureaucratic identifications more important than religious identifications. To the question "To what degree, if any, does purchase of service endanger an agency's program or impair its autonomy?" 354 administrators stated in an overwhelming majority that purchase of service as a policy is sound for their agencies; only 5 percent see extremely harmful effects to their agency programs. As with subsidy, it is the Jewish agencies that are least disturbed by the practice.

Table 8 shows the different attitudes that welfare administrators bring to a consideration of purchase of service when they consider it against the background of the ideological question of church-state separation and against the background of the very practical question of the threat that purchase of service might pose to the autonomy of their agencies. It is obvious that the chief concern is not a church-state principle, but a fear that their agencies' autonomy

[22] Episcopal children's institution, New York.
[23] Episcopal children's institution, Ohio.
* Detailed results of this aspect of the study may be found in Appendix V.

will be jeopardized. In this matter of purchase of service the incidence of concern for agency autonomy is far higher than it is for the violation of church-state separation. This change of concern is most marked among the Catholic agencies: only 1 percent of their agencies see any problem of church-state principle, while 33 percent see a problem of agency autonomy, and for another 8 percent the problem is considerable. None, however, see an extreme danger. A similarly sharp difference obtains with the nonsectarian agencies: only a few see any problem of church-state principles, but nearly half see at least some problem of agency autonomy.

TABLE 8. *Agency Attitudes toward Purchase of Service and Church-State Separation, as Compared with Attitudes toward Purchase of Service and Agency Autonomy, by Affiliation*

Denomination	Church-State Separation		Agency Autonomy	
	Total Number of Agencies	Purchase of Service Some Violation, Percent	Total Number of Agencies	Purchase of Service Some Threat, Percent
Protestant	136	40	137	53
Nonsectarian	64	28	67	46
Jewish	58	19	58	29
Catholic	91	1	92	41
Total	349	24	354	45

The breakdown of the Protestant responses to the question of church-state separation versus purchase of service shows great variation among the denominations.* The Southern Baptists are the least favorable to purchase of service. American Baptists and Evangelical and Reformed are generally undecided as to where the line of church-state separation in welfare should be drawn. Lutherans, Episcopalians, and Methodists decidedly favor purchase of service.

Notwithstanding these variations, the overall policy thinking of the agencies sampled in this study is decidedly in favor of purchase of service. Of all the agencies 89 percent have no doubt that sale of service to government is compatible with their principle of church-state separation, and 85 percent have no doubt that sale of service is compatible with the autonomous control of their agencies.

* See Appendix V for a breakdown by denomination.

PROTESTANT AGENCIES

The church-related agency has two main concerns in the maintenance of its autonomy: administrative control and characteristic
ideology. The comments of Protestant welfare administrators reflect
a deep awareness of these two concerns. The administrative control
must remain within the agency even if necessary supplementary
funds come from outside the agency. The dilemma created by such
a situation—common to all three principal denominations—was expressed thus by one Episcopal administrator: "We all realize that
we are on a 'socialist kick,' and I feel this is taking direct responsibility away from the people. But on the other hand how many
agencies would fail if it weren't for tax funds?" [24]

A Methodist speaking from twenty years of experience in government welfare programs considers both subsidy and purchase of
service as extremely dangerous to agency autonomy:

If a health or welfare agency directly receives tax funds it is accountable
to and is controlled by Government to an undesirable and damaging
extent. Limited governmental control is good in some situations but it
shackles freedom of thought and action.[25]

Another Methodist, also speaking out of his experience, came to a
similar conclusion:

There are private agencies in some parts of the country which are almost
100% financed by public agency payments. The danger here is that the
private agency loses its identity as a private agency. For instance certain
Protestant institutions for children are 90–100% public financed. Their
sponsoring churches no longer have more than token interest in the work
of their institutions. The institutions have essentially given up control
over their services.[26]

That some churches have only "token interest" in welfare stems
from the social-role conception the churches have of themselves.
Where social philosophy accentuates an indirect and remote involvement of the church in the social order, the church's interest
in welfare is probably no more than a gesture. Where this philos-

[24] Episcopal home for the aged, New York.
[25] Methodist home for the aged, New York.
[26] Methodist children's home, Missouri.

ophy prevails, it is probably inevitable that administrative control of services will slip from the church.

This brings us to the second concern, the characteristic ideology. Where sponsoring churches have more than "token interest" in their institutions or agencies, they want both motivation of the staff and climate of the agency to reflect church ideology. This form of welfare, where motivation and climate reflect the church, is known in Protestant theology as *diakonia*, which means a service out of love, or "a ministry of service." Some Protestant leaders feel that this ministry is weakened when it is financed by government funds. Donald Howard, former dean of the University of California at Los Angeles School of Social Work, framed the question:

If the church is to get into semi-commercial ventures, selling services to government for a price, why not admit its true nature and not pretend that a "ministry of love" and "service"—which government pays for—fall within so noble a concept as *diakonia?* [27]

Reasoning on the basis of this question, some argue for services entirely free of involvement with government. Speaking of dangers in a purchase-of-service policy, one director said: "The greatest danger is a philosophical or theological one—namely, the agency becomes dependent on the tax dollar and loses its identity as an institution which is motivated and sustained by love." [28]

Another administrator quotes figures to prove the reality of this danger. His agency, a children's institution, has an extensive purchase-of-service program, charging government agencies from 80 percent up to full cost of service. The agency's total budget is $221,703, of which $133,277, or 60 percent, is tax funds. Speaking of the effect that purchase of service has on the ideological character of his institution, he said,

In our instance I feel that the agency is functioning as an arm of the public units and has little ideology of the type usually associated with sectarian agencies. I feel that dependence upon tax funds has hindered the development of a practical working ideology.[29]

[27] Letter from Donald S. Howard to the former executive director of the Department of Social Welfare, National Council of the Churches of Christ, April 2, 1959.   [28] Lutheran hospital, Colorado.
[29] Episcopal children's institution, Michigan.

Unlike the group discussed above, most Protestants distinguish between purchase of service and subsidy and do not regard purchase of service as a threat to agency autonomy; like the group above, they base their opinions on experience. In the words of one administrator: "Based on our experience of more than forty years, we see no encroachment of authority on the part of City or State." [30] A maternity home in New York that in 1960 received from the local government $55,589, or 64 percent of its total budget, summarized its experience: "Our agency has always had excellent relations with our own county and outside county agencies." [31] A Lutheran director summarized the experience of his hospital, which has received several Hill-Burton grants and since 1930 has received a percentage of its budget from county funds: "This is well-integrated; and through practice has demonstrated no conflict with ideology of this hospital." [32]

Some executives believe that the amount of tax funds should be held to a specified percentage of total budget. If tax-fund assistance is kept to a minimum, the agency's policies are not seriously affected:

So long as the tax funds we receive are very much less in total than the private funds, our policies are clear and tolerable—and the purchase of services by the tax supported groups is clearly a contractual, year by year arrangement.

This agency, which receives from the local government 15 percent of total budget, summarized its experience: "(1) The agency principles are upheld, (2) the agency is challenged by these new demands to resistive clients, and (3) people are helped that could not otherwise be helped." [33]

CATHOLIC AGENCIES

On the relation of subsidy and purchase of service to Catholic agencies, the comments of local executives center around three propositions: (1) one function of government agencies is to

[30] Methodist hospital, Maryland.
[31] Episcopal maternity home, New York.
[32] Lutheran hospital, Minnesota.
[33] Episcopal children's services, New York.

strengthen, not compete with, voluntary agencies; (2) neither purchase of service nor subsidy violates church-state separation; (3) subsidy is distinguished from purchase of service because of the different effect of each on the agency's administration and hence on its autonomy. Catholic agencies will be considered in the light of these three propositions.

The social-philosophy principle on which much of Catholic agency policy is based, the principle of subsidiarity, has been explained in Chapter 3. On the local agency level, this principle forms the basis of policy. It was expressed by a Missouri executive:

> I see the role of the public agency as making possible the maximum level of service provided by voluntary associations, sectarian and nonsectarian. I do not see that this money is a promotion of the religion. I see it as a promotion of service to people by voluntary initiative in those areas of responsibility which have not yet been completely delegated to the public authority by reason of scope, magnitude, or other causes which would make it no longer feasible for the voluntary agencies to attempt to supply the service in question.[34]

One Wisconsin administrator provided a case study of his agency, where the principle of subsidiarity had held and was in recent years revoked—to the enervation of the agency's program. This enervation was due in part to the Wisconsin law relating to foster care which, according to Ruth Werner, "excludes from state reimbursement those placements made by courts or county administrative agencies with voluntary agencies."[35] This law tends to "discourage court commitments to voluntary agencies except on a selective basis."[36]

The purpose of the legislation was to distribute more equitably among state and county governments the cost of foster-care services. The law has achieved this end, but it has also been responsible for financial pressures on voluntary agencies. According to the law, "If the county takes the commitment or assumes the legal custody of a child and places it or purchases care in a voluntary or private institution, the county cannot be reimbursed by the state."[37] Thus,

[34] Catholic children's service, Missouri.
[35] Werner, *Public Financing*, p. 34. [36] *Ibid.*
[37] Director of Catholic Charities, La Crosse, Wis., memorandum, n.d. (Mimeographed.)

the county is penalized financially if it uses voluntary-agency facilities.

In the opinion of a director of a Wisconsin children's agency, this legislation has had two unfavorable effects. It strictures the parent, for he "no longer has a choice except a public agency," [38] and it penalizes the voluntary agency. To substantiate this second point, the director cited the history of his budget during the past five years. In 1956 the agency received from governmental agencies $41,728, or 26 percent of total annual expenditures, as reimbursement for services for the year. Most of these funds came from the county. By 1959 reimbursement had dropped to $32,791, or 17 percent of budget. In 1960 reimbursement funds dropped again, to $13,717, or 7 percent of total expenditures. The county was purchasing hardly any services from the agency, and the future held no promise of any purchase of service by government: "For all intents and purposes we have no money anticipated for 1962 as partial reimbursement for foster care from counties." [39]

To a Catholic welfare administrator this Wisconsin case is an example where the principle of subsidiarity, though applicable, is not applied. The voluntary agency offering the same service as the government agency finds itself competing unfavorably with the government agency because it is financially at a disadvantage. According to the director, the diminishing reimbursements are due not only to Wisconsin's foster-care law but also to some of the local government's "individual administrators who seek a one-agency (public) concept." [40] According to this director, the one-agency concept is a "serious trend," since the "public welfare (one-agency) concept has at the present time almost eliminated voluntary agency services where public funds are used or inability to pay for service is determined." [41]

The Wisconsin administrator was supported by a California colleague, who wrote of the same failure of government welfare to utilize voluntary effort where it exists. In his judgment, voluntary

[38] Letter to the author from a director of Catholic children's services in Wisconsin, July 27, 1961.   [39] *Ibid.*

[40] Letter to the author from a director of Catholic children's service in Wisconsin, June, 1961.   [41] *Ibid.*

agencies are in financial straits because some government agencies refuse to utilize available voluntary services. Unless something is done, all social service

will become a government monopoly. Agencies are being trapped between inflationary costs and restricted income, which is being limited in no small degree by excessive taxes at every level of government. The government does not compete unfairly with private enterprise in business even in matters relating to national defense and national security. It should not compete unfairly with private enterprise in the field of meeting human needs.[42]

The second proposition concerns subsidy and purchase of service in social welfare in relation to the separation of church and state. Unlike many Protestants, who distinguish subsidy from purchase of service in their consideration of church-state separation, Catholics make no distinction and regard neither subsidy nor purchase of service as a violation of church-state separation as they understand it. In the words of a Connecticut director, "The principle of separation is not at stake." [43] And a New York administrator said,

Patients themselves are tax-payers. . . . There is little if any difference in the use of public funds by sectarian agencies and nonsectarian agencies. They both have the same operating costs to meet and they both serve the same public—the American people.[44]

The administrator of a children's institution conducted by an order of Catholic sisters reversed the question and asked in effect, "Who's subsidizing whom?":

We recently figured the subsidy of the Sisters' salaries (donated) to the State of Oregon at over $80,000 a year. We have no conflict about accepting state aid to assist us in work with troubled children, who are served on a nonsectarian basis.[45]

Certainly some Catholics would tend to the opinion that the very nature of a sectarian agency, far from meriting exclusion from reimbursement for services rendered, might entitle the agency to re-

[42] Catholic children's services, California.
[43] Catholic children's institution, Connecticut.
[44] Catholic hospital, New York.
[45] Catholic children's institution, Oregon.

imbursement. They would argue that where a child, for example, has a right to be cared for, he has likewise a right to be cared for in a sectarian agency if his needs are best met there. In the words of a Minnesota director: "Actually this is the right of the citizen to have provided the appropriate service which he needs. Often that appropriate service is best obtained through a private agency." [46]

But on the question of what constitutes appropriate service that is reimbursable from tax funds, the Catholic answers seem to fall into three categories: all social services, including religious, strictly social services, and services to meet only physical and material needs.

One diocesan director, whose definition of reimbursable services included not only social but religious services as well, said: "An agency that provides service should receive reimbursement for its services including the religious phase which is part of Catholic service." [47] This all-inclusive definition had been, as will be shown later, repudiated several years previously by top-level Catholic executives.

The Catholic administrators holding the most common view fall in the second category. In the words of one administrator: "The service purchased is social service." [48] And another said, "Our services to the child and his family are professionally oriented. Direct religious services are extra and do not add to the cost of care. The child's need for service is the same no matter what his religion." [49]

As will be shown later in this study, the second definition of reimbursement by tax funds—strictly social services—is today most commonly held by both Catholic and Protestant administrators.

The third definition of reimbursable services, as proposed by some administrators, would seem to be restricted. It excludes professional social work services and is limited to physical and material needs. An Ohio administrator states the practice of his agency flatly: "The tax funds are used for the material benefits of the boy." [50] A Wisconsin director outlined the position of his agency in greater detail:

[46] Catholic children's services, Minnesota.
[47] Catholic children's services, Ohio.
[48] Catholic children's services, California.
[49] Catholic children's institution, Connecticut.
[50] Catholic children's institution, Ohio.

Our basic philosophy is that since it is generally accepted that government has responsibility for the physical necessities of people in need (public assistance), government ought to pay for the physical care for all who receive care from us; but that spiritual care, i.e. that which relates to the spirit (mind and will) should not be jeopardized by government payment. We, therefore, will raise our own funds to pay for casework, education and religious training of our clients.[51]

The third proposition held by Catholic administrators is related to their distinction between subsidy and purchase of service. This distinction, they declare, is made not because of any violation of church-state separation but because of administrative considerations and the possible threat to the agency's program. A Wisconsin director makes this distinction clearly: "We see no church-state conflict as to either kind of payment insofar as political or religious ideology is concerned. We oppose lump-sum payments for administrative, casework and equity reasons." [52] And a California agency said,

Contractual agreements for purchase of service or matching fund grants for specific types of services can be negotiated in our opinion in a satisfactory manner. Outright subsidy for general purposes of the private agency program would open the door to internal controls which would weaken private agency initiative and structure.[53]

A Minnesota executive's analysis reveals considerable reflection on the matter, distinguishing between the relationship that obtains in a contract involving subsidy and the relationship in a contract involving purchase of service:

In giving a private agency a subsidy, a paternal relationship would be present which might tend to develop into a supervisory role on the part of the public agency. In purchasing service public agencies are receiving a definite value for the dollar, and are merely consumers of our product.[54]

Not all Catholic directors are equally convinced of the necessity to distinguish subsidy from purchase of service with respect to their effects upon a voluntary agency program. Catholic agencies par-

[51] Catholic children's services, Wisconsin.
[52] Catholic children's services, Wisconsin.
[53] Catholic children's services, California.
[54] Catholic children's services, Minnesota.

ticipating in the study form two main groups. The first group comprises 39 diocesan offices of Catholic welfare. Each of these offices is headed by a priest, who is appointed by the local bishop and is diocesan director of social welfare. Generally each of these offices conducts both children's and family service programs and many also conduct other affiliated services and institutions. The second group comprises 68 other administrators, some of whom head agencies that are under the administrative authority of a diocesan director and some of whom are outside that authority. The administrators in this group are either lay people or members of religious orders. And the participation of each in this study was independent of the first group.

Both groups of Catholic administrators regard purchase of service as a sound policy, there being only a very small number from each group that sees purchase of service as constituting a considerable danger to the autonomy of Catholic agencies. But the two groups do not agree on the danger that subsidy constitutes for their agencies (Table 9). The nondiocesan directors see subsidy as involving

TABLE 9. *Attitudes of Diocesan and Nondiocesan Agency Directors toward Subsidy and Purchase of Service*

Degree of Danger to Autonomy	Purchase of Service		Subsidy	
	Nondiocesan	Diocesan	Nondiocesan	Diocesan
None	32	22	16	5
Some	16	14	11	8
Considerable	6	2	11	9
Extreme	. . .	. . .	. . .	3
Total	54	38	38	25

hardly any more risk to their agencies' programs than purchase of service. The diocesan directors do not look so favorably on subsidy, half of them considering it as a risk they are not willing to take. They are much more cautious about subsidy than the lay directors. Indeed, they have considerably more reservation about subsidy than do Jewish directors and are about as cautious as Protestant directors where agency autonomy is concerned. A possible explanation of these differences and similarities may be the comparatively large-scale and complex administrative operations of diocesan welfare departments, which would make diocesan directors more acutely aware of the administrative problems involved in subsidy and more eager to avoid them.

Jewish agencies, like most Protestant and Catholic agencies, need money. The Federation of Jewish Philanthropies of New York City, where government support is readily available, spoke of its need and of its successful partnership with government as an appropriate way of meeting the need:

If we are to hope to meet the full need as anticipated, we must look for increased support from public welfare sources.

The progress achieved in service to children has demonstrated beyond doubt the values of the partnership between voluntary and public agencies.[55]

A similar viewpoint was expressed by the former Commissioner of Social Security when he warned the Council of Jewish Federations and Welfare Funds that the Jewish agencies could "no longer take a position that seems to bar grants, but must measure both grants and purchase of care payments by the general tests of accountability, standards, community need, agency independence, and so forth." [56] Other Jewish spokesmen, reasoning along similar lines, think that since their agencies are so pressed financially and since the purchase of service from voluntary agencies is less costly to government than similar services would be if offered directly by government, Jewish agencies have "an obligation to seek government aid where it is available, and to press for increased grants." [57]

In spite of their need and the exhortations to seek and accept tax funds, the Jewish welfare community has been severely criticized by some of its own members for its entanglement with government agencies. Taylor fears that a shift in the political climate

[55] Federation of Jewish Philanthropies of New York, *To Serve the Children Best*, p. 43.
[56] Schottland, "Use of Public Funds by Jewish Agencies," p. 10.
[57] Selig, "Implications of the Use of Public Funds," *Journal of Jewish Communal Service*, XXXVI, No. 1 (Fall, 1959), 58.

could leave high and dry any voluntary agency that is dependent on government funds.[58] Or, as Perlman indicates, a change in the social climate may lead the government to make excessive demands on tax-supported voluntary agencies:

Government already has some control of policy through its licensing and inspection roles, its setting of personnel standards. If there is extensive need for service to a non-Jewish group is there not a possibility that government might press our agencies for such services? [59]

The substance of these fears is expressed in the frequently quoted words of Morris and Gurin:

The rationale for maintaining a voluntary service loses a good deal of its force if it operates as a conduit for governmental services and financing. At some point, the question must arise whether and in what way this indirect service should give way to direct service by government through public institutions.[60]

In spite of warnings and criticisms from leaders in Jewish welfare, local directors seem convinced that fears about government involvement are groundless. Among sectarian groups the administrators of Jewish agencies have the least fear that their programs will be endangered by subsidy or purchase of service. Whatever may account for this confidence, Jewish agencies seem to have lost nothing by accepting either Hill-Burton or child welfare funds, as Selig points out:

The hospitals which have used government funds report their experiences rewarding in every respect. In contrast to some misgivings in anticipation, government domination and interference were not experienced and hospitals continued to operate without infringement of their autonomy.[61]

[58] Taylor, "The Impact of the Changing Federal Welfare Program on Jewish Communal Activities," *Jewish Social Service Quarterly*, XXXI, No. 1 (Fall, 1954), 45.

[59] Perlman, "Effect of Increased Public Funds on Jewish Federations and Agencies," *Journal of Jewish Communal Service*, XXXIV, No. 1 (Fall, 1957), 22.

[60] Morris and Gurin, "Community Relations Implications in the Use of Public Funds by Sectarian Agencies," *Journal of Jewish Communal Service*, XXXIII, No. 1 (Fall, 1956), 50–51.

[61] Selig, "Implications of the Use of Public Funds," *Journal of Jewish Communal Service*, XXXVI, No. 1 (Fall, 1959), 50.

In those children's institutions receiving tax funds, Selig notes, "Jewish mores, customs and milieu are upheld" and the acceptance of non-Jewish children "does not alter the specific character of the agency." [62]

This study made clear the positive stand of Jewish welfare administrators on church-state cooperation in welfare. The attitudes of the Jewish directors on church-state separation do not differ markedly from the attitudes of the Catholic directors.* This attitude runs counter to the commonly accepted American Jewish church-state attitude, which has been in general one of strict separation of church and state. Leo Pfeffer, leading Jewish expert on church-state issues, considers the use of tax funds for sectarian purposes "immoral" and "unconstitutional." In his opinion "taxation is compulsion," and therefore "the use of tax-raised funds, that is, funds raised by compulsion, for any but secular purposes is tyranny and a corruption of religion." [63]

Although nonwelfare groups like the American Jewish Committee, the American Jewish Congress, and the National Community Relations Advisory Council have asked the Jewish community not to relax the absolute application of the principle of church-state separation, representatives of the Jewish welfare community approve the Hill-Burton program, their reason being that it does not infringe on the sectarian character of Jewish hospitals.[64] The conflict between financial need and the principle of church-state separation may give rise to confusion about which way to go. In 1952 the American Jewish Committee lauded the Jewish community for its alertness to church-state matters in education but chided

---

[62] *Ibid.*, p. 52

* For this data the reader has already been referred to Appendix V.

[63] Leo Pfeffer, "Commentary on Church and State Relations in Social Welfare," in Methodist Church, *Research Consultation on Church and State*, Third Assembly, Chap. IV, p. 26.

[64] Selig, "Implications of the Use of Public Funds," *Journal of Jewish Communal Service*, XXXVI, No. 1 (Fall, 1959), 50. The Jewish Community Relations Advisory Council has generally taken no formal position against tax funds for sectarian welfare programs. Individual staff members of the Council strongly oppose the practice, but the official attitude of the Council seems to be one of caution joined to a desire for further study.

social workers for sluggishness on church-state matters in the field of welfare. After research on the reports of the annual conferences of social workers, the Committee criticized the profession because it did not consider "the church-state issue and its impact in the welfare field." [65] Hence, the Committee assumed the task of "sensitizing social workers to the limits of cooperation between the sectarian agency and government." [66]

The American Jewish Congress is a staunch church-state separationist organization, and the tenor of its statements implies that the principle of separation is absolute. As recently as 1955, however, when the AJC presented to a subcommittee of the U. S. Senate a statement on "Freedom of Religion and Separation of Church and State," no mention was made of welfare. The statement outlined five areas where, according to the AJC, Americans give only lip service to the principle of church-state separation: (1) religious instruction and observance in public schools, (2) use of tax funds for religious education and use of governmental property for religious purposes, (3) enforcement of compulsory Sunday laws, (4) "restrictions on the erection of houses of worship and religious schools in new residential communities," and (5) prohibition of the adoption of a child by persons of a faith different from that of the child's natural parents.[67]

Nothing was said of lip service to the principle of church-state separation in health and welfare, where hundreds of millions of Federal, state, and local government dollars go annually for the construction of sectarian institutions and for the costs of sectarian services.

From the above evidence of Jewish nonwelfare ideology and the attitudes of Jewish welfare directors, it is clear that Jewish welfare practice is not consonant with other Jewish thinking. Many grass-roots directors reject the ivory-tower theorizing of nonwelfare organizations. In response to a paper presented by a spokesman of the National Community Relations Advisory Council, in which the program coordinator of the Council strongly advised Jewish

[65] Saveth, "Religion and the Welfare State," p. 24.   [66] Ibid., p. 25.
[67] American Jewish Congress, "Freedom of Religion and Separation of Church and State," Congress Weekly, XXII, No. 33 (November 28, 1955), 12.

welfare agencies that accepting tax funds was both anticonstitutional and perhaps even immoral, Jacob Kravitz, the Executive Director of the Jewish Federation in Dallas said: "My concern . . . is not in relation to theoretical community relations problems . . . but rather in relation to the pragmatic considerations of community organization experience." [68] Kravitz apparently expressed the mind of many administrators:

This is the significant *Fact*—that there *is* no legal impediment. . . . Nowhere has there been any substantial acceptance by the courts that the use of public funds by sectarian welfare agencies violates the practice of Church-State separation.[69]

While many civil rights leaders and community relations organizations caution the Jewish community against accepting tax funds, most welfare executives and administrators see little reason for concern and go along with the new trend which Schottland characterizes as "the partnership of voluntary and public agencies." [70] Local directors apparently adhere to this concept of partnership. With few exceptions they affirm that the principle of church-state separation is not involved in the acceptance of tax funds. Their comments, some of which are given below, reflect the rationale of their church-state policies.

Some administrators state categorically that this sort of negotiation with government, even involving subsidy, is no violation of church-state separation. In the words of one administrator: "I believe in the separation of church and state, but subsidy to private agencies by government does not violate the Constitution." [71] Another administrator stated the case as do some Protestants and Catholics, drawing down policy from two basic principles: (1) "Children who meet the eligibility requirements for government aid are entitled to it without regard to their faith"; (2) "Statutory law and/or general practice, based on predominant community sentiment, require that a child in need of substitute home care be placed

---

[68] Kravitz, "Comment: What Price Public Funds?" *Journal of Jewish Communal Service*, XXXVII, No. 1 (Fall, 1960), 123.

[69] *Ibid.*, p. 121.

[70] Schottland, "Use of Public Funds," p. 3.

[71] Jewish children's services, Texas.

in an environment of his own faith if available," and in conclusion, "If a child eligible for government aid is in need of substitute home care, there is no reason why government cannot provide care by purchasing it from existing sectarian facilities rather than having to duplicate them." [72]

A second group of Jewish directors qualify their approval of tax funds for sectarian agencies. They make a double distinction by reason of which funds could be justified in some cases and disallowed in others. The first distinction is between a church-related and an ethnic-related welfare institution. The following statement by an administrator in Georgia makes this distinction clear: "One must first distinguish between a sectarian agency sponsored by an ethnic group and one sponsored by a church. A Jewish agency is quite different from a Catholic-controlled agency." [73]

Another seemed to be getting at the same distinction in saying that a sectarian agency does not qualify for tax funds because of its ideological moorings:

I see no violation where there is no ideological and no exclusive practice in the service rendered. Each agency service would need to be examined to make this determination. To the extent that there were such, I would see violation.[74]

This introduces the idea of a voluntary agency that is sectarian but at the same time disavows any ideological base or purpose, a present matter for debate among Jewish welfare leaders. Those opposed to a sectarian agency that professes no ideological base ask: What is left of a Jewish agency if its functioning is not characterized by Jewish ideology?

The Georgia administrator who made the first distinction—between church and ethnic welfare agencies—also made the second distinction—between welfare agencies and educational institutions:

Social welfare services should not be equated with the parochial education and church controlled programs. Health and social welfare agencies meet broad human needs which quite often are unrelated to church dogmas or catechisms.[75]

[72] Jewish children's services, Missouri.
[73] Jewish children's services, Georgia.
[74] Jewish hospital, Ohio.
[75] Jewish children's services, Georgia.

Another made the same distinction with reference to purchase of service: "There is no violation as long as we are not a religious educational group." [76] Still another pointed to two different church-state traditions, one obtaining in welfare and one in education:

I have . . . considerable question about subsidizing public aid to education. Historically it appears to me, that health and welfare services have originated and developed along sectarian lines and the support of them for a good long while, at least, could be basically constructive. The reverse seems true re education.[77]

It is noteworthy that not one Protestant or Catholic local director who answered questions pertaining to church and state in welfare made any reference to church and state in education, but several of the Jewish administrators introduced the matter of education although they were questioned only about church-state issues in welfare.

In addition to those who approve categorically of tax aid to sectarian welfare and those who make the above distinctions, there is a third group of Jewish administrators who would extend the principle of church-state beyond the field of welfare and others who would even revamp the principle altogether. One agency had to face the distinction between education and welfare in a practical case. The agency is an institutional treatment center for children with a $230,779 budget, of which $79,356, or 34 percent, is received from tax funds. The director stated that the agency favored both purchase of service and subsidy, although he himself considered subsidy to be "some" violation of church-state separation. The situation with which the agency was faced was similar to the case discussed previously, *Sargent* v. *Board of Education*,[78] which was contested in New York in 1904.

By his statement of his own viewpoint and of his agency's resolution of the situation, the director exemplifies one of the problems of this third group of administrators:

There are circumstances under which, in my opinion, payments would violate the church-state separation principle. Such circumstances have so

[76] Jewish children's services, Indiana.
[77] Jewish home for the aged, Washington.
[78] 177 N.Y. 317, 69 N.E. 722 (1904).

far not come up for us except in one respect: in our operation of our own school for a select number of our children. In this case we have sought public funds.[79]

The administrator, who was apparently overruled by his board of directors, seems to be saying discreetly that the action of his agency was, in his opinion, a violation of the principle of church-state separation.

That there is a strain between principle and practice is obvious. While it is not obvious how severe the strain is, at least one administrator thinks that the church-state principle should be revised. His agency favors the "partnership" policy advocated by Schottland and a broader interpretation of the church-state principle. The agency's budget is $336,412, of which $113,104, or 39 percent, is tax funds. Speaking to the broader concept of church-state in our society, the administrator said,

A classical interpretation of "church-state" relationship is no longer relevant or helpful. While religious auspices may sponsor services, religious auspices cannot possibly develop the complex of highly professional resources required to execute sectarian responsibilities.[80]

This administrator is both thinking and acting in terms of a new church-state principle. Many Jewish welfare administrators who are still acting on the traditional interpretation of church-state separation are nevertheless thinking along lines of the above proposal.

CONCLUSIONS

Although there are broad ranges of practices and attitudes among the welfare agencies of the three religious groups, the following generalizations seem to obtain:

Unlike the Protestant welfare executives, Catholic and Jewish welfare executives generally consider the subsidy of sectarian welfare agencies as no violation of church-state separation.

All three religious groups are more fearful over the effect that subsidy would have upon the autonomy of their agencies than they are concerned over subsidy as a violation of church-state separation.

[79] Jewish children's institution, California.
[80] Jewish children's services, Pennsylvania.

There is almost unanimity among Protestants, Catholics, and Jews that purchase of service does not violate the principle of church-state separation. Within the Protestant denominations especially, however, there are contradictory attitudes even about this form of cooperation between government and sectarian welfare. These attitudes fall along a continuum from complete rejection of this form of church-state cooperation to complete acceptance of it.

Protestant agencies manifest greater policy indeterminacy than Catholic or Jewish agencies, as manifest in the conflicting policies within the denominations. The broad range of policies reflects the search among Protestants for a compatible church-state principle.

Protestant agencies, especially of the "free-church" tradition, face a twofold struggle in adjusting to social change: the struggle to bureaucratize the church's structure and the struggle to preserve the purity of religious ideology while adjusting to a new pattern of relationship with government. Indication of the struggle was succintly expressed by the Southern Baptist administrator in Missouri whose hospital accepted tax funds: "We are opposed in principle, but recognize we must live under the laws of the land."

Catholic agency administrators generally reflect the church's accepted social philosophy principle of subsidiarity, which sees government as an enabler to voluntary effort.

The practices and attitudes of Jewish welfare administrators concerning church-state separation is similar to those of Catholic administrators. In spite of the admonitions of Jewish civil rights and public relations groups, Jewish welfare executives have little fear that cooperation with government and the receipt of tax funds either compromises church-state separation or endangers the autonomy of their agencies.

7

NEW PRINCIPLES FOR OLD

By NOW it is clear how influential in determining the role of the churches in modern social welfare are the three themes—power, individual responsibility, and religion and social control—referred to in Chapter 2. Social change is forcing the churches to reevaluate their role in the welfare state and to adjust their social philosophies and policies to the new society. In the face of the growth of government power, the churches sense a need for a more permanent institutionalized form of church structure that will be viable in a society of institutionalized power. In the face of diminishing personal responsibility for the social order, the churches sense a need for voluntary "organic groups" through which the individual may carry out this responsibility. In the face of increased secularism, the churches sense a need to assume a more direct responsibility for social institutions so that society may reflect the churches' character.

That the churches are adjusting to the social change is indicated by their frequent meetings to formulate social policy, their efforts to organize services along more structured lines, and a growing attitude among them of cooperation between government and the church. Realizing that the role of the state is bound to be more inclusive, religious leaders are revising their former policies of absolute separation of church and state as obsolete in today's society. Practically speaking, for the field of social welfare, cooperation with the state means that the church uses the tax power of the state for sectarian welfare programs. While not all churches are sure they want to embark on such a policy, some have already reinterpreted the principle of church-state separation in terms of this type of cooperation.

By far most of the discussion of the church-state problems that are involved in determining the role of voluntary welfare and its relationship to government has been carried on by the Protestant churches. The purpose of this chapter is to explore Protestant policies on church and state as that principle is understood in the field of social welfare and to indicate what seems to be the trend in the practice of church-state separation.

Among top Protestant welfare leaders there is considerable unanimity as to certain policy practices, purchase of service, for example. But, as Kelley indicates, there is no agreement on an overall church-state policy: "Protestant organizations and agencies do not have a clearly defined rationale of church-state relations." [1] This is not to be wondered at. Since Protestantism is highly decentralized, difference in policy is inherent in its structure. Neither the National Council of Churches nor the national departments of the individual Protestant denominations have policy-making authority; their responsibility is only advisory. Nevertheless, Protestant leaders want "to develop a consistent and constructive position," [2] and are concerned when they see local-level welfare administrators adopting policies and practices that have far-reaching church-state implications. Frequently the practices of two local agencies within a denomination are in conflict with each other, and both are at variance with the thinking of national administrators.

Although the same may be said with reservations of Catholic and Jewish local policies, nevertheless, local Catholic and Jewish agencies have a more recognized anchor to which they adhere. The Council of Jewish Federations and Welfare Funds, which meets at least once a year, exerts a certain amount of influence on the formation of Jewish welfare policy. And although Catholic welfare policies differ from diocese to diocese, there tends to be far greater agreement on policy among Catholics because of the influence of the episcopal board of directors of the National Catholic Welfare Conference and the National Conference of Catholic Charities,

[1] Kelley, *Questions of Church and State*, p. 28. [2] *Ibid.*

which meet at least once a year for policy purposes. This consensus among Catholic welfare executives was alluded to by the former executive secretary of the Department of Social Welfare of the National Council of Churches: "Only the Roman Catholic Church seems to have maintained a relatively consistent philosophy in relation to social welfare programs." [3]

It is especially important for non-Protestants to understand the extreme theological and social philosophy differences that exist among Protestant denominations. It is inaccurate to lump all denominations under the category "Protestant." Actually there is closer theological kinship and a greater degree of social-philosophical unity between certain Protestant churches and the Catholic church than exists among the rest of the Protestant denominations taken together. This is said not only because the author has observed it to be a fact, but also because some Protestant welfare executives have been anxious that this point not be blurred.

ORIGINS OF POLICY DIFFERENCES

A Protestant denomination's teaching on the nature of church and state conditions to a great extent that denomination's stand on welfare policy.

From the time of the Reformation, the Protestant churches have been split into what Sweet calls a right-wing, conservative group and a left-wing, radical group.[4] The founders and the great reformers of the great Protestant state churches which sought to maintain close church-state relations were conservatives. The Lutheran principle was that both church and state are divinely established orders and therefore the church must maintain an uncritical attitude toward secular authority. This forced the church into the shadows of society and turned over the great problems of national and social life, politics, economics, arts, and sciences to their own devices. This is the reason, according to Mueller, that "Lutheran ethics tended to become Quietistic and therefore ineffective in the

---

[3] Villaume, "Church-State Relations in Social Welfare," p. 2.
[4] Sweet, "The Protestant Churches," *Annals*, CCLVI (1948), 43–46.

stream of life." [5] The Calvinistic principle was that the power of the state is at the service of the church in order to enforce both a temporal and a spiritual law. Such a philosophy is workable, if at all, only where there is an established religion.[6] Since it could not work in America, church and state went their separate ways. The American social milieu was quite inimical to both theories of church-state cooperation.

But it was friendly to "left-wing" Protestantism. The left-wing group is made up principally of those radical elements which in the sixteenth and seventeeth centuries were known as Anabaptists, offshoots of Calvinism. They protested against ecclesiasticism and insisted upon the almost exclusively personal character of religion. In Chapter 3 we saw how this theology made the churches resistant to institutionalization. Their resistance to institutionalization made them equally resistant to any form of church-state cooperation. To the left-wing groups and the many revivalist movements which they fathered, the American social climate was especially favorable. Because revivalist theology and American democracy were so compatible, the sects in the United States grew out of all proportion to the churches of the right-wing.[7]

Generally speaking, a particular view of church-state separation will depend on where one stands with reference to a left-wing or a right-wing theology. At the present time there are three types of Protestant welfare policy—or three phases of policy development—that hinge on the principle of church-state separation.

POLICIES OF SEPARATION

In extreme left-wing Protestantism there is no lack of clearly defined church-state policy. In this extreme group, frequently referred to as the "free" church, are found the absolute church-state separationists,[8] which include the young organization called Protestants and Other Americans United for Separation of Church and State (POAU). Although POAU originally endorsed a principle of total

---

[5] Mueller, *Church and State in Luther and Calvin*, p. 69.   [6] *Ibid.*, p. 128.
[7] Sweet, "The Protestant Churches," *Annals*, CCLVI (1948), 43–46. See also Troeltsch, *Protestantism and Progress*, pp. 123–27.   [8] *Ibid.*

and absolute separation, it has in recent years spoken more of a "friendly separation."[9] Nevertheless, POAU vigorously opposes tax support for any church-related service, however public in function it may be. In the opinion of C. Stanley Lowell, leading spokesman of the organization, there is "one decisive test," on which the American principle of separation of church and state may be evaluated—money: "Any church seeking tax money for its operations is endeavoring to breach the wall of Church-State separation."[10] For the most part the consideration of absolute church-state separation is theoretical; in practice it is maintained by only 5 percent of the welfare agencies. Most Protestants see this absolute separation as having been perhaps practicable in other times but unrealistic today, as the experience of health and welfare agencies of all denominations testifies.

POLICY INDECISION

As we move away from the extreme left, we encounter more complex considerations—multiplicity of policies, indecision about policy, and contradiction of policy and practice. The churches' uncertainty about the relationships they wish to maintain with the state is exemplified in several areas. One of these areas is the armed-forces chaplaincy program. Baptists and Seventh-Day Adventists regard chaplains' participation in the armed forces as a violation of the separation of church and state. Nevertheless, Baptists, especially Southern Baptists, greatly exceeded their quotas in the chaplaincy program, in which hundreds of their ministers were supported by tax funds for work that is necessarily of a sectarian character. For a Baptist such a situation is a matter of moral principle which he must reconcile with Lowell's one decisive test of separation—money. As one representative at the Methodist's New York East Conference observed: "One of the church executives responsible for his church's participation in the program, as a bow to principle, refuses to accept reimbursement by the government for travel done at the request of the government."[11]

[9] Lowell, *Separation and Religion*, p. 9.   [10] *Ibid.*, p. 13.
[11] Marion J. Creeger, "The Military Chaplaincy," in Methodist Church, *Research Consultation on the Church and State* (Third Assembly), Part I, p. 11.

Another area of uncertainty is church participation in the Social Security program. For many of the free-church groups, coverage of church ministers and church employees under a government insurance program was originally considered a violation of church-state separation. Many at first refused to accept coverage either for themselves or for their employees. Discussions on whether or not the churches should participate in the Social Security program evoked from one former Protestant welfare official the following comment:

The uncertainty of the American churches with regard to the relations they desire to maintain with the state became abundantly clear when they were confronted with the opportunity for participation . . . in the Federal program of Old Age, Survivors, and Disability Insurance.[12]

When this question was debated by churchmen, "arguments about church and state were often difficult to sustain or refute."[13] In time, many revised their evaluation of the program's compatibility with church-state separation. Although the free church tends to have a smaller coverage than the larger episcopal and presbyterian types of churches, most of the groups have a high coverage. Two large denominations, Baptists and Methodists, have 40 and 51 percent participation, respectively. This almost equal division between those who elect and those who reject coverage would seem to indicate the division of opinion that still exists among the churches as to what their relationship with government should be. Those issues that are still debated in the free churches seem to have been resolved by the established churches.

The Hill-Burton Act created another area in which the churches could test their policies on church-state separation. From the beginning the Southern Baptist Convention and most of its state conventions "have consistently opposed acceptance of government money by their hospitals and homes."[14] As recently as 1959 the American Baptist Convention passed the following resolution: "We object to the use of tax funds for the benefit of sectarian institutions, including schools and hospitals, and the use of tax-concession for the benefit of church-controlled commercial enterprises."[15]

---

[12] Villaume, "Church-State Relations," p. 27.   [13] Ibid.

[14] Kelley, Questions of Church and State, p. 29.   [15] Ibid.

Further severe condemnation of the acceptance of Hill-Burton funds by sectarian hospitals came from the Baptist Joint Committee on Public Affairs, a common organization of the American and Southern Baptist Conventions: "The most flagrant violation of the principle of church-state separation is the government's allocation of funds to build church-operated hospitals, as provided for in the Hill-Burton Act." [16] Yet, as we have seen, some of the hospitals of these two groups accept Federal funds.

Although there is this conflict between top-level censure of government assistance and local acceptance of grants, there is also an awareness of the conflict. One national American Baptist executive told the author, "We are full of inconsistencies." He noted as an example the American Baptist schools in India which accept funds from the British government for their educational programs. He also noted the Congo, where funds are received from the Belgian government for the same purposes. The church "justifies," he said, these policies because the circumstances in these countries demand such policies. If the American Baptists did not conduct schools, there would be no schools in those areas. The Southern Baptists, he added, have acted on the same policy in the southern part of the United States, where they have accepted millions of dollars for university dormitory construction.

Those who speak of "the hesitancy of Protestant groups to seek or accept federal funds" [17] must from the foregoing facts in our study be aware that this hesitancy is not universal. Segments of some denominations hesitate to seek or accept government funds and as a matter of principle ultimately reject such funds, but these segments are small and are growing smaller. Segments of all denominations seek and accept government funds. If it is true, as the Baptist Joint Committee on Public Affairs stated, that "the most flagrant violation" of church-state separation in the use of tax funds to build church-operated hospitals, [18] then all churches violate the principle. Perhaps it is more accurate to say that social change is bringing about a reevaluation of the principle. Some of the delegates to the National Council of Churches Conference on Policy and Strategy

[16] Baptist Joint Committee on Public Affairs, *Review and Evaluation.*
[17] *Ibid.*   [18] *Ibid.*

made this point in terms of the church's role in society: "The involvement of the church in society has caused them to violate this principle in practice." [19] It is this involvement that is responsible for the current reexamination, reevaluation, and redefinition of the principle of church-state separation for modern society.

INFLUENCING ISSUES

Before discussing the third phase in the relationship of church and state in welfare policy, at least some mention should be made of the churches' attitudes toward two social issues. The present status of these issues affects greatly the policies of church-related welfare, and current changes in policy cannot be understood unless the issues are understood. We have presented these issues in Chapter 2 from a sociological point of view as themes underlying the basic question of this study. Here we shall merely record the churches' attitudes toward them.

Growth of Government

The first issue is the tremendous growth of government welfare, which the churches regard as a threat to their role in welfare. Protestant and Catholic leaders alike have formally expressed their concern. The administrative board of the National Catholic Welfare Conference pointed to the threat with specific reference to children's services: "It is a source of growing concern to us that in certain parts of our country there is a trend to regard this whole field of foster care as falling within the exclusive province of governmental authorities." [20] In an address to the Thirty-fifth National Conference of Catholic Charities, the Most Rev. Bartholomew J. Eustace, Bishop of Camden, stated that the government welfare program is "both a good and a desirable thing," but cautioned: "Anything . . . can be purchased at too high a price." Bishop Eustace is afraid that if we are not careful about the way that welfare

[19] National Council of Churches, *Policy and Strategy in Social Welfare*, p. 43.
[20] "The Child: Citizen of Two Worlds," in *Our Bishops Speak*, p. 164.

services are provided, "we may someday awake to find ourselves with perfect social security, but without a vestige of liberty."[21] Msgr. John O'Grady, a former Executive Secretary of the National Conference of Catholic Charities, voiced concern for the continued existence of Catholic welfare: "How can voluntary agencies survive in the face of huge bureaucracies?"[22]

Like Catholics, Protestant welfare conferences have marked the threat that an expanding welfare state poses to the role of the church in society. The Lutheran World Conference on Social Responsibility reported: "Almost universally in the culture of western civilization . . . the state has risen to a place of almost overwhelming dominance."[23] The report contends that by this dominance the state has assumed functions previously performed by the church and has thus rendered these church functions superfluous or at best ornamental.[24] In a similar context the delegates to the historic Cleveland Conference on Social Welfare sponsored by the National Council of Churches warned: "The competence of the state in the field of social welfare should be continuously examined, so that the role of the state may be appropriate."[25] The Conference expressed the fear that continued growth of state welfarism "will inevitably mean governmental control of church-related institutions."[26] The Conference on Policy and Strategy of the National Council of Churches was similarly alarmed: "The enlarged role of government in this field creates serious problems in the relation between church and state."[27]

Growth of Secularism

The second issue is related to the first; it concerns the growing secularism of social institutions, which many think is due at least in

[21] Eustace, "Charity, Industry and the Welfare State."
[22] O'Grady, "Implications of the Proposed Public Assistance Program," p. 1.
[23] "The Christian Individual and His Role in Groups" (group discussion), in National Lutheran Council, *Christ Frees and Unites*, p. 90.
[24] Anders Nygren, "The Contexts within Which the Church Develops Responsible Service," in National Lutheran Council, *Christ Frees and Unites*, p. 45.
[25] Bachmann, ed., *The Emerging Perspective*, p. 153.   [26] *Ibid.*, p. 74.
[27] National Council of Churches, *Policy and Strategy*, p. 26.

part to the principle of church-state separation as it is understood and applied in this country. The original Protestant intent of church-state separation was, according to Limbert, "to break down the division between sacred and secular" by assigning to the state a sacred function, a religious and moral responsibility. In this way, it was hoped, society would be infused with religious significance. "In many respects, the reverse has happened and one area of human activity after another has become secularized." [28] Troeltsch was of the same mind: the state is less and less a "religious institution" that counts among its functions "the protection of the Christian commonwealth and the moral law," [29] and society is more and more characterized by secularism. And in Glock's evaluation,

There is a growing body of opinion, as yet largely unorganized, postulating an essentially humanistic philosophy over against a theistic one. Its influence on American life has already been manifested in the marked reduction in the functions served by the established churches in such areas as education, social welfare, and recreation.[30]

Some in our society regard the "secular state as a corollary of religious pluralism," [31] and for them the secular state is a valid principle of a pluralistic society. Such a society should minimize the social functions that are to be carried out by the church. Others think that a secular state portends the establishment of a kind of religion of secularism. Whatever it may be, some authors refer to secularism as a religion.[32] The reaction of the Lutheran Conference came in the words of the Most Rev. D. Volkmar Herntrich, Evangelical Lutheran Bishop of Hamburg: "When man is seen apart from any bond with God, man himself is made God." [33] This concept of self may be of individual man or social man. Idolatry is the deification of objects which man has made. The objects of deifica-

[28] Paul M. Limbert, "Toward a Protestant Philosophy of Child Welfare," in Protestant Conference on Child Welfare, *The Nation's Children*, p. 20.

[29] Troeltsch, *Protestantism and Progress*, p. 106.

[30] Glock, "Issues That Divide: A Postscript," *Journal of Social Issues*, XII, No. 3 (1956), 41.

[31] F. Ernest Johnson, summary of statement in *The Nature of Religious Pluralism*.   [32] Lowell, *Separation and Religion*, p. 22.

[33] D. Volkmar Herntrich, "The Nature of Man and His Destiny, According to the Christian Faith," in National Lutheran Council, *Christ Frees and Unites*, p. 39.

tion may be material things or social institutions: "the deification of the state . . . , the deification of a race or a people—or of an ideology from which these things all receive their value." [34] Purely secular states are self-destructive, Bishop Herntrich warned, because they are based upon purely humanistic systems. And further, speaking from painful experience, he said, "humanistic systems take on anti-humanistic tendencies." [35]

Catholic bishops, too, have on many occasions scored secularism. In their judgment the interpretation of the principle of church-state separation has been radically twisted beyond usefulness, and the principle itself has been used as "the shibboleth of doctrinaire secularism," [36] which the bishops see as bent on destroying all co-operation between government and organized religion. The delicacy of church-state problems in a pluralistic society has been exploited "to the detriment of religion and good citizenship." [37] The bishops are confident that this "concrete problem, delicate as it is, can, without sacrifice of principle, be solved in a practical way when good will and a spirit of fairness prevail." [38] This spirit of fairness the bishops spelled out in the following way: "cooperation involving no special privilege to any group and no restriction on the religious liberty of any citizen." [39]

This kinship of Protestantism and Catholicism is shifting the poles of religious tension. Speaking of this kinship against the growing body of secularism, Glock observes:

There are already signs that Catholic and to a lesser extent Protestant and Jewish action is being devoted increasingly to counteracting these tendencies. It is conceivable that the result may be to shift the focus of attention from interreligious to religious-secular tension.[40]

The modern religious dialogue is well-known. Churchmen of widely disparate denominations are seeking common elements of religion and morality that may serve to ground a society as pluralistic as ours. Dialogue on theology and morality is difficult because

---

[34] *Ibid.*, pp. 39–40.   [35] *Ibid.*, p. 41.
[36] "The Christian in Action," in *Our Bishops Speak*, p. 151.
[37] *Ibid.*, p. 150.   [38] *Ibid.*   [39] *Ibid.*, p. 153.
[40] Glock, "Issues That Divide: A Postscript," *Journal of Social Issues*, XII, No. 3 (1956), 41–42.

in these areas there are widely extreme divergencies, but dialogue on the level of social philosophy and policy is less difficult. Catholics have taunted Protestants for allowing social institutions to lose their religious character. Protestants have taunted Catholics for their aloofness from the stream of secular society. Wherever the burden of taunt, one prominent Protestant notes that Catholics are "more ready to close ranks now with other church related agencies than at any time in the past." [41] In 1948 the Catholic bishops issued a statement in which they professed their eagerness to cooperate and pointed out how in their judgment these two issues—secularism and the growth of state power—are associated:

We stand ready to cooperate in fairness and charity with all who believe in God and are devoted to freedom under God to avert the impending danger of a judicial "establishment of secularism" that would ban God from public life. For secularism is threatening the religious foundations of our national life and preparing the way for the advent of the omnipotent state.[42]

Both Protestants and Catholics seem to realize that if they compete rather than cooperate in the field of social policy, they would increase social tensions and aid the growth of secularism. In the words of Yinger, "Religious concern for political decisions can promote the value integration of a society only to the degree that diverse religious groups emphasize common values." [43] To promote this integration as far as possible, Protestant and Catholic welfare leaders have for several years been carrying on—with success—a continuous interdenominational dialogue on social-welfare policy. Four meetings are held annually, usually in New York, where Protestant and Catholic representatives are guests of the Department of Social Welfare of the National Council of the Churches of Christ. In April, 1958, at the first of these informal conferences, Msgr. Raymond J. Gallagher, the present secretary of the National Conference of Catholic Charities, stated the purpose of the dialogue:

The position occupied by sectarian services . . . is of such importance that we feel a careful definition of position would lend strength to the

41 Villaume, "Church-State Relations," p. 34.
42 "The Christian in Action," in *Our Bishops Speak*, p. 151.
43 Yinger, *Religion, Society and the Individual*, p. 251.

cause. To divide and conquer has often been the technique used by those who wish to eliminate a formidable opponent. We feel that the forces of religion are likely to be put in this position unless a common ground is found upon which to take a stand. We are well aware of the theological differences which exist among us. It is not our intention to engage in a discussion of these. Rather, it is our hope from these conferences a solidarity of thought might be developed regarding the role of sectarian welfare services.[44]

This statement is a call to reassessment in order "to validate the philosophy of sectarian services," [45] but more significantly it is a call to churches to unite against those forces that would deny to the churches a direct involvement in welfare service and a participation in the formation of social policy. In the face of something that is more threatening and has potential far beyond the field of welfare, controversy and feeling on theological differences are set aside. "We cannot stand by," Msgr. Gallagher said, "permitting such influences less valid and less traditional to take to the attack against us." [46]

These issues are not only lessening interdenominational tensions but bringing about harmony of thought on social-policy matters. And underlying this trend is the reconsideration of a viable principle of church-state separation in the welfare field. This reconsideration will become more evident in the discussion of the third phase of church-state policy-making in welfare.

POLICIES OF COOPERATION

If some churches are living through the phase of welfare-policy indecision characterized by the hiatus between policy and practice, other churches have already narrowed the gap. Indeed, some of these go well beyond church-state considerations in the field of welfare and speak to a more fundamental and far-reaching principle of church-state separation. To exemplify this third phase, we have selected two large denominations, Methodist and Lutheran, which have studied and debated the matter and adopted policies favorable

---

[44] Gallagher, statement before a meeting of Protestant and Catholic welfare leaders, p. 1.   [45] Ibid.   [46] Ibid., pp. 1–2.

to their members. To supplement these two examples, we shall discuss in the same framework the activities of the National Council of Churches.

Methodists

For some time now Methodists have been encouraging the acceptance of Hill-Burton grants. This quasi-policy is based on "Church and State Relations," a formal letter written on June 15, 1951, to the Board of Hospitals and Homes of the Methodist Church by Bishop William T. Watkins, President of the Board. The letter is significant because it carries the principle of church-state separation beyond the field of welfare and gives the principle equal application in a wider context.

In the opinion of Bishop Watkins, a large group of government activities should be lumped together. In this group, in addition to construction grants for denominational institutions, should be included tax exemption of church property, the chaplaincy program in the armed forces, the appointment of chaplains to the House and Senate of the United States, and the use of the motto "In God We Trust" on our money. Of the items in this group Bishop Watkins says, "If anyone of them be declared unconstitutional, the whole group ultimately goes out together." In Bishop Watkins' opinion, however, none of them is unconstitutional, and cooperation of church and state in welfare and in other areas should be encouraged. Speaking in the framework of this wider application of the church-state principle, he says:

It does not appear to me that our American doctrine of the separation of the Church and the State requires that the government shall not be helpful to the churches, but only requires that the government shall not favor one church above another, nor do I conceive that our American philosophy requires that the churches not be helpful to the government, but only that no church shall seek to secure the establishment of itself as an official State church.[47]

The import of this letter is vast. The Board of Hospitals and Homes of the Methodist Church directs more homes and hospitals

[47] Quoted in Kelley, *Questions of Church and State*, pp. 28–29.

than any other board cooperating with the Welfare Department of
the National Council of Churches, and "in the absence of an official
Methodist Statement this letter has been an unofficial guide for the
staff of the Methodist Board from 1951 to date." [48] After extensive
study, the legal counsel for the Methodist Episcopal Hospital in
Philadelphia concluded that nothing in Methodist policy was inimical to the acceptance of Hill-Burton funds. The Executive Secretary of the hospital explained the policy in the tone of Bishop Watkins' letter: "I believe that the Church and the State can, and ought
to, work together for the common good of all." [49] H. Burnham
Kirkland declared that the obsolete principle of absolute separation
must yield to the principle of cooperation:

> It appears that there are times when "cooperation" between church and
> state are absolutely necessary in order to protect the positive free exer-
> cise of the rights of the church. Furthermore, this "cooperation" is good
> for the state, perhaps even more than for the church, because it signal-
> izes the high place given to religion and there is much to be said for the
> state's going out of its way to encourage voluntary associations of citi-
> zens which are important for the welfare of the community.[50]

Accordingly, the 1960 Methodist Conference rejected the inflexibility of "free-church" Protestantism. In the thinking of the
conference, this inflexibility arises from a misinterpretation of the
principle of separation. The traditional American church-state principle is a "political principle under which whatever pertains to a
man's religious choice and convictions and observance must be pre-
served absolutely free as possible of any external pressure, force or
coercion by the State." [51] The Conference therefore rejected the
concept of "separation of church and state," labeling it a left-wing
theological contrivance, which was at least archaic and at worst
extreme:

> This concept of the "secular" or "laic" or "doctrinally-neutral" State
> is an American institutionalized invention, following clues offered by the
> Anabaptists and the rationalists and others. It has developed under the
> formula or slogan "separation of church and state"—a term which is too

[48] Villaume, "Church-State Relations," p. 30.
[49] Methodist Church, *Research Consultation on the Church and State*, Fourth
Assembly, Part III, p. 9.   [50] *Ibid.*, pp. 24–25.   [51] *Ibid.*, p. 4.

rigid in some respects, too loose in others. A more definitive formula might be *"separation of faith and coercion!"* [52]

The impetus given to social policy by Bishop Watkins' letter has in recent years gained such momentum among Methodists that some of them have spoken of extending the principle of church-state co-operation beyond the area of welfare to education. The Secretary of Health, Education, and Welfare, addressing the college presidents assembled at the meeting of the National Association of Methodists Schools and Colleges, suggested that the provisions of the Hill-Burton Act be extended to include loans for instructional buildings, libraries, and laboratories. His suggestion was heartily applauded. From this approval Ralph Decker, the Director of the Department of Secondary and Higher Education of the Methodist Board of Education, assumed "that the Methodist College Presidents are ready to accept such aid!" He summarized the Methodist attitude:

The sentiment seems to run that we should not accept governmental funds for current expenses in our schools, but that we can accept funds for building purposes, for if the government attempts to use this money as a lever for controlling the school, we can say, "If you don't like the way we run the school you can come down and take your library off our campus." [53]

Methodist educators share the financial embarrassment of all private-school educators. One Methodist educator put the matter unequivocally: "If we're going to stay in business at all and keep the private independent schools from disappearing, we are going to have to accept this (government) aid." [54] Perhaps the success that Methodists have experienced with the acceptance of Hill-Burton grants gives weight and confidence to the policy of wider application of church-state cooperation.

Lutherans

Basic to Lutheran social philosophy is a concept of both the church and the state as "divinely appointed institutions serving

[52] *Ibid.*   [53] *Ibid.*, p. 8.   [54] *Ibid.*

fundamental needs of mankind." They therefore "stand in a position of mutual subordination and superordination," and each serves "areas of primary and areas of secondary responsibility." By this route Lutheran social philosophy arrives at a basic principle in welfare. The American Lutheran Church "reaffirms its conviction that church and state may well cooperate in rendering welfare services." [55] An extreme and inflexible concept of church-state separation is foreign to Lutheran ideology:

Governmental agencies are looked upon by Lutherans as partners. A Lutheran understanding of the separation of church and state does not rule out the reality of partnership in serving people who are both Christians and citizens. Particularly in welfare, Christian and secular social concerns overlap.[56]

The Board of Christian Social Action of the American Lutheran Church considers "dangerous" those who think that the American principle of separation "means divorcing all state-related functions from any God-relatedness and relegating religion to an incidental or inconsequential matter, the concern only of sectarian partisans." [57]

Lutheran health and welfare executives are far from accepting "free-church" views of church-state separation. In fact, they hold that government assistance to sectarian welfare effort should be extended to include aid for institutional chapels, office space and equipment, clerical assistance, and salaries for spiritual ministries. According to the Board of Christian Social Action, the government's providing for these things "is compatible with the proper relationship of church and state to each other in their responsibility to the total person so long as the organized church bodies alone are privileged to determine the ecclesiastical standings of the chaplains

---

[55] "Aims and Purposes of the American Lutheran Church in Its Program for Christian Social Action," a statement prepared by the Board for Christian Social Action, American Lutheran Church, and adopted by the American Lutheran Church in convention assembled, Fremont, Ohio, October 7–14, 1948 (Columbus, Ohio, Board for Christian Social Action, 1948).

[56] Bachmann, ed., *The Activating Concern*, p. 62.

[57] Board for Christian Social Action of the American Lutheran Church, *The Christian in His Social Living* (Minneapolis, Board for Christian Social Action, 1960), p. 88.

so serving." [58] Obviously, Lutheran social welfare thinking goes far beyond that of denominations which have reservations about participating in the armed-services chaplaincy program or hesitate about coverage under Federal Social Security.

In 1958 the Board of Christian Social Action extended the principle of church-state cooperation beyond the field of welfare into the field of education. In the matter of education the Board accepts the principle that "funds raised through taxation for public education should be used only in support of publicly controlled education." [59] It also accepts, however, the distinction made by the Supreme Court in the 1899 *Bradfield* v. *Roberts* [60] welfare case, that the individual is distinguished from the institution which provides him the service. In 1958, therefore, the Board extended the principle of church-state cooperation to the field of education and based its policy on this distinction: "A church school may accept for the benefit of its pupils any governmental benefits which accrue solely to the individual without regard to his status as a student." [61]

Like most new ventures, this endorsement enjoined caution. The Board recognized that it is sometimes difficult "to separate the acceptable from the unacceptable forms of state benefits." It recommended, therefore, that the church not accept government benefits "when it is not clear what is within permissible limits." [62]

National Council of Churches

Although the National Council of the Churches of Christ has no authority to set policy for its member churches, its conferences and activities influence the thinking of the churches. The tone of many of these conferences is that the church-state philosophy of "free-church" Protestantism has not been without ill effects, and the stress is repeatedly towards maintaining the God-relatedness of society and the state.

[58] *Ibid.*
[59] *Ibid.*, p. 79.   [60] 175 U.S. 299 (1899).
[61] *Ibid.* In essence this is the position and line of reasoning maintained by many Catholics. See Virgil C. Blum, "Freedom of Choice in Schools," *Homiletic and Pastoral Review*, LVIII, No. 1 (October, 1957), quoted previously.
[62] *Ibid.*, p. 88.

The 1955 Cleveland conference studied specific matters in relation to church and state. When the Section on Health and Medical Care discussed the Hill-Burton Act, it recognized that some denominations consider that the act is "a clear subordination of the church-related agency to the state and is, *ipso facto*, wrong." [63] Notwithstanding this opposition, the official report of the Section stated: "We believe that it is not contrary to the traditional relationship of the church to the state to accept Hill-Burton funds." [64]

The same Section discussed purchase of service with special reference to those local and state governments that prohibit purchase of service from sectarian institutions on the ground that such transactions violate the principle of church-state separation. The Section disagreed with this interpretation of the principle: "We believe there is no valid reason for such limitations on the purchase of health services." [65]

On the national welfare level the thinking of most Protestants and Catholics is similar. At an informal meeting (held in New York on September 17, 1958) made up of several representatives of the National Conference of Catholic Charities and representatives of seven Protestant denominations, purchase of service was discussed exhaustively. In the minutes of the meeting it is recorded that "there was complete agreement" that church-related institutions have a right to accept such payment for services. It was reasoned that the acceptance of tax funds is for social services and that, where the social worker performs a religious ministry, it is "an additional service not paid for by public funds. . . . This was differentiated from 'proselytizing!' " [66]

In a private interview with the author, one of the delegates pointed out that originally the Protestant executives opposed purchase of service because they thought that the Catholic interpretation of that form of government assistance extended to the purchase of crucifixes, vestments, chapel supplies, and the like. Only when the Catholic executives cleared up this misunderstanding and it became evident that purchase of service meant the same thing to Cath-

---

[63] Bachmann, ed., *The Emerging Perspective*, p. 73.
[64] *Ibid.*   [65] *Ibid.*, p. 74.
[66] *Resume—Meeting of Roman Catholic and Protestant Welfare Leaders.*

olics and Protestants was there unanimous agreement on this practice as sound policy.

This informal conference of Protestant and Catholic leaders had
been preceded by the historic National Conference on Policy and
Strategy in Social Welfare, convened by the National Council of
Churches in Atlantic City, N.J., in 1957. In an effort to go beyond
discussion of specific problems and take some preliminary steps
toward the formulation of welfare policy, the official delegates to
the conference agreed unanimously on the following statement:

The Churches and church-related agencies cannot avoid relating to government both in the formulation and enforcement of laws and in the
administration of public agencies.
  Cooperation by church and state for the good of the citizen and community need not compromise the integrity of either.[67]

When the question arose of what a policy like this would mean
to church-state separation, the delegates urged "that the principle
of separation of church and state be so interpreted as to make possible the voluntary cooperation of the churches and the agencies of
government on a nondiscriminatory basis." [68]

For Protestant churches especially this is a new course and a long
way from the "absolute separation" and the "wall of separation"
language generally associated with the church-state principle.
Yinger points to a search that has been gaining momentum particularly since 1917—a search for a common ground of unity for
American society. One aspect of the search has been consensus on
religion and on the religious foundations of the nation, and the area
of concentration of this search has been a satisfactory definition of
the principle of separation of church and state.

Traditional arguments for absolute separation stress greater freedom for church and for state, and it is argued that each profits by
this separation. The advantage to the church is that it escapes direct
political domination and is thus freer to criticize political processes
and power structures. The advantage to the state is that it is more
flexible and less encumbered when not linked to an ecclesiastical
structure. In Yinger's judgment, however, the evidence does not

[67] National Council of Churches, *Policy and Strategy*, p. 17.
[68] *Ibid.*, p. 26.

support this argument, for the church's freedom from political power structures raises the question of the powerlessness of the church in society.[69]

This is the dilemma the churches face: to be free from the state is to be weakened in political influence; to be institutionally united with the state is to be a mere political functionary. "It is perhaps the recognition of this dilemma," says Yinger, "that has been partly responsible for recent reduction in the sharpness of separation of churches and state in the United States." [70] The trend is therefore rather in the direction of what Yinger calls "the cooperation of churches and state." [71]

It is likely that Yinger's recognition of the new direction of the principle of separation is based not only on the present emphasis of churchmen on cooperation rather than on a "wall of separation," but also on a changing attitude evidenced in some Supreme Court decisions. In the New Jersey school-bus case the Court interpreted the First Amendment to mean that "Neither a state nor the Federal Government . . . can pass laws which aid one religion, aid all religions, or prefer one religion over another." [72] The prohibition against aiding "all religions" created a stir and caused a good deal of resentment.

In the New York released-time case several years later, the Court seemed to take another attitude toward the relationship between the government and religion:

The First Amendment . . . does not say that in every and all respects there shall be separation of Church and State. Rather it studiously defines the manner, the specific ways, in which there shall be no concert or union or dependency one on the other. This is the common sense of the matter. Otherwise the state and religion would be aliens to each other—hostile, suspicious, and even unfriendly. Churches could not be required to pay even property taxes. Municipalities would not be permitted to render police or fire protection to religious groups. Policemen who helped parishioners into their places of worship would violate the Constitution. Prayers in our legislative halls; the appeals to the Almighty in the messages of the Chief Executive; the proclamations making Thanks-

---

[69] Yinger, *Religion, Society and the Individual*, p. 250.
[70] *Ibid.*, p. 251.   [71] *Ibid.*, p. 248.
[72] *Everson* v. *Board of Education*, 330 U.S. 1.

giving Day a holiday; "so help me God" in our courtroom oaths—these and all other references to the Almighty that run through our laws, our public rituals, our ceremonies would be flouting the First Amendment. A fastidious atheist or agnostic could even object to the supplication with which the Court opens each session: "God save the United States and this Honorable Court." [73]

Having stated the basic philosophy of recognition and cooperation between religion and the state, the Court then addressed itself to the area of cooperation specific to the case—education:

We are a religious people whose institutions presuppose a Supreme Being. . . . When a state encourages religious instruction or cooperates with religious authorities by adjusting the schedule of public events to sectarian needs, it follows the best of our traditions. For it then respects the religious nature of our people and accommodates the public service to their spiritual needs.[74]

That such cooperation will continue and will increase in the field of social welfare seems very likely. One instance of this trend toward cooperation was the recent recommendation of the Advisory Council on Child Welfare Services. When in 1959 an amendment to the Social Security Act extended coverage to child welfare services in urban areas, some voluntary welfare representatives were alarmed by the proposed expansion of government services and requested that a citizens' committee study the matter.[75] The committee endorsed the extension of Federal responsibility to share in the cost of all government child-welfare programs. But—significant for our context here—it made further recommendations:

The Council believes that public and voluntary agencies should join ranks to make use of all available resources to improve services to children. It also endorses the principle of purchase-by-service by the public agency from qualified voluntary agencies wherever needed. Such services should be purchased on a case-by-case, cost-of-care arrangement.[76]

Charles Schottland, the former Commissioner of Social Security,

[73] Zorach v. Clauson, 343 U.S. 306.   [74] Ibid.
[75] Wickenden, "Social Security and Voluntary Social Welfare," Industrial and Labor Relations Review, XIV, No. 1 (October, 1960), 103.
[76] U.S. Senate, Report of the Advisory Council on Child Welfare Services, U.S. Department of Health, Education, and Welfare, Social Security Administration, 86th Cong., 2d Sess., December 28, 1959, document No. 92 (1960), p. 6.

sees in these trends a decided reversal of past policies. In the 1940s the accepted policy still bore the cast of the days of Harry Hopkins: public funds should be spent only by public agencies. By 1960 there was a change, Schottland observed, not only in policy but in the philosophy underlying the policy. That public funds may be spent by private agencies subject to the standard-setting authority of the public agencies is accepted as sound policy today. That the new policy is being adopted is evidenced by the expenditure of public monies by voluntary agencies. The increasing number of church-related services is further indication of the growth of this trend.[77]

The national sectarian executive with whom the author has conferred have expressed their approval of this trend and their intention to work for its continuance and growth. It can be expected, therefore, that cooperation between church and state in welfare will increase. Whether, and if so to what extent, this policy of cooperation of "the churches and state" will characterize other areas of church-state relationships cannot at this time be conjectured.

[77] Schottland, "The Relationship of Public and Private Agencies." The foregoing paragraph is a synopsis of Mr. Schottland's lecture.

8

SUMMARY AND CONCLUSIONS

THE prime movers in the change from a simple to a complex society were the economic and industrial revolutions, and our present highly institutionalized social order is the child of those revolutions. As technological superseded nontechnological methods and new economic systems replaced laissez-faire, a revolution in social institutions became inevitable. It has fallen to the twentieth century to cope with the many aspects of these revolutions, and the aspect with which we have here been concerned is the pattern of social welfare—the resources that are available and the resources that are created to meet social needs. Two agents in that pattern are voluntary welfare and government welfare—the former old and the latter comparatively new. An analysis of the policies underlying the role of each and their relationship in our society cannot be made without a consideration of three social variables, or three themes, confronting the policy-makers: the dynamics of political power, personal freedom and individual responsibility, and the social control function of religion.

In democratic societies individual freedom is an unquestioned value. Although the role of government power in a democracy has been less conspicuous in the past, in recent years this power is also an unquestioned value. The dilemma for democratic governments is how to use power and assume responsibility for the social order, and yet leave the individual free and make him responsible for himself and for the social context of his life. Modern society is of necessity cast in a state-welfare mold, which diminishes individual responsibility and extends government authority. In some areas government needs even more power than it now possesses, but the process whereby government exercises power and assumes its concomitant responsibility sets into motion an internal dynamism toward a power structure that renders difficult the function of individual responsibility. In this way democracies generate within themselves what Mannheim calls "self-neutralizing factors" that are their own undoing.[1]

To maintain the necessary balance between personal freedom and government power, between personal responsibility and government responsibility, voluntary welfare executives recognize the need to build into the social structure machinery by which the individual retains responsibility for himself and for the social institutions in which he participates. This responsibility can no longer be carried directly by the individual; it must be fulfilled through the voluntary associations with which he identifies himself and in which he is able to maintain his identity in society. Voluntary action both cushions and stabilizes the relationships between the individual and government.

The third theme that confronts policy-makers in this matter is religion and the control function it exercises in society. A realization that religion adds to voluntary action another sociological dimension vital to social unity is discrediting and reversing previous policy assumptions of many social philosophers—that a pluralistic society must be a secular society.

There seem to be two main reasons for this reversal from secularism as the ideal for a pluralistic society. First, a secular society runs the risk of achieving only a superficial social unity. There is a growing awareness that the unity that arises from social control must be based on something more meaningful than secular custom and law. A society that lacks internal unity based on conscience eventually disintegrates. When this internal form of social control is not performed by religion, some other institution, usually the state, assumes that function, in which case the state ultimately becomes an absolute. The presence of state absolutism in the world is causing

---

[1] Mannheim, *Sociology of Culture*, p. 174.

the churches to examine themselves and identify their social roles. Churchmen are turning away from previous notions of that role which would have the church only remotely involved in the affairs of society and tend to see the church as having a more direct responsibility for the social order.

Second, a secular society cannot meet the most basic human needs. It may stave off social and economic insecurity, which are only part of the general insecurity, but more prevalent and far more harmful are psychological and spiritual insecurity.[2] A society without a "transcendental religious foundation"[3] will fall short of this goal.

With an eye to the sociological and theological implications underlying these themes, sectarian leaders of welfare associations are reexamining the role of the churches in welfare. They are summoning the churches to greater responsibility for direct professional health and welfare services. If Protestant leaders previously considered the church's involvement in social action to be aimed only at instructing and motivating the individual, today there is more talk of an institutionalized form of social action aimed at establishing Protestant services that will remain under the control of the churches. To help the churches provide these services, funds from government agencies are becoming increasingly available, and the agencies of all churches—Protestant, Catholic, and Jewish—are taking advantage of them.

No legal issue is directly involved in the principle of church-state separation, since there is a long legal history of government aid to sectarian health and welfare services. In determining our church-state principle, the courts have long distinguished government aid to sectarian welfare from government aid to sectarian education. Tax support is a violation of church-state separation in one field—sectarian education—but no violation in the other—sectarian welfare.

Nevertheless, some church leaders think that such a distinction cannot be maintained in practice, since tax aid to sectarian welfare is another facet of the wedge that eventually will open up to tax aid for sectarian education. Welfare policies, in their opinion, should be evaluated before the same tribunal as policies in education. Un-

[2] Mannheim, *Freedom, Power and Democratic Planning*, p. 301.
[3] *Ibid.*, p. 289.

derlying this attitude is the fear that as the welfare state continues to grow, characterized by policies of government support for sectarian welfare, these policies will reverberate onto other areas of public life and so come to characterize the basic relationship between church and state. These leaders are a minority and are generally not involved directly in social welfare.

To most welfare administrators the ideological issue of church-state separation is not a crucial concern. Confronted with ideological objectives against government assistance to sectarian welfare, the reaction of administrators is generally hard-headed and realistic. By acknowledging the constitutionality of tax support for sectarian welfare, the courts have marked off the areas of the church-state issue. Recognizing the position of the court, one administrator said concerning tax support for sectarian agencies, "This is the significant *Fact*—that there *is* no legal impediment." [4] Accordingly, Catholic and Jewish administrators regard even the subsidization of their agencies as compatible with the principle of church-state separation.

While most Protestant administrators will not go so far, they do join Catholics and Jews in favoring capital construction grants and purchase of service, seeing in these practices no violation of the principle of church-state separation. Convinced that their sectarian services are superior to or at least as good as government services—except for the availability of money—most sectarian leaders recommend that government assist their agencies with tax funds.

Thus, most sectarian hospitals receive large construction grants, and most sectarian welfare agencies have contractual agreements whereby they receive government funds on a purchase-of-service basis. Some agencies of all denominations receive government funds, and in some cases these funds represent well over one-half of the total agency budget. Many agencies are thus enabled to release other funds for the expansion of programs.

Two interesting phenomena accompany this widespread practice. First, in spite of the fact that they receive tax funds, most agencies state that they have no policies about receiving or not receiving government aid. The paradoxical fact is that, apparently without

[4] Kravitz, "Comment: What Price Public Funds?" *Journal of Jewish Communal Service*, XXXVII, No. 1 (Fall, 1960), 123, quoted previously.

realizing it, they have very significant policies of accepting government funds.

Second, in many cases these government contracts conflict with the policies of higher church leaders. As we have mentioned, many church leaders have endorsed a "hands-off" policy, indicating to their constituents the danger and even immorality in receiving tax monies. While other church leaders are not so conservative as to endorse a "hands-off" policy, still they vacillate, unable to determine the role of the church in modern society and what relationship they would like to see their agencies maintain with government.

Meanwhile, local agencies are pressed with other than ideological determinations and are making their own decisions and determining their own practices. In either case—whether regardless of the policy indetermination of church leaders or whether in spite of their disapproval—local administrators are accepting government funds and are thus evolving from the local level policies that have far-reaching implications.

All these developments point to a new trend in church-state policy. These two streams of influence—church leaders for ideological reasons readapting church policy to the changing social order, and agency administrators for pragmatic reasons determining church policy by actual cooperation with government—are converging to recast the traditional policy of church-state separation.

In the first stream, top church executives approach the question of the relationship of government to voluntary agencies from a consideration of the role of the church in society. This approach involves theological considerations of the nature of the church, but it also involves sociological considerations like the impact that social change and the social structure have on the church. It is becoming increasingly clear that an individualistic approach alone, which does not involve the church more immediately in determining social policy, is out of tune with the present social structure. In direct language this means that the churches recognize their need to bureaucratize and to become more directly involved in the social order, so that in a bureaucratic society they may successfully withstand the threat that secularism poses to the purpose of the church.

The second stream is made up of administrators of church welfare institutions who are competing for the welfare dollar and finding government a cooperative partner. If they have ideological doubts about the wisdom or morality of church-state cooperation in welfare, these doubts are being dispelled by their own success in working with government and by the tacit approval that church leaders generally give to use of tax funds by church agencies. This success is building their confidence to the point of questioning the viability in the new society of a principle of church-state separation, at least as it has been understood in the past.

In the field of social welfare these two forces seem to be driving toward a new interpretation of the church-state principle. Contemporary social structure is so expanding and complex, with state welfarism taking such a sweeping hold, individual responsibility is proportionately so diminishing with the costs of welfare and other services frequently so beyond individual control, and secularism is so challenging the social role of the churches that many consider the traditional interpretation of the principle of church-state separation as no longer relevant in today's society. Therefore many church leaders and welfare executives are reevaluating and reinterpreting the principle in terms of cooperation of church and state on the basis of equality of the churches and the state.

9

GUIDELINES FOR PUBLIC POLICY

ONE thing emerges from this study: the churches need to determine their role in social welfare and the policies that will direct their relationship with government. Pragmatic considerations are significant determinants of social welfare policy, but even they need to be evaluated against a background of a thought-out philosophy of social welfare. In the long life of a civilization the latter is at least as important as the former. In the light of this study and taking into consideration both pragmatic determinants and ideological values, I should like to propose a framework of social welfare policy that bears upon the relationship between government and voluntary welfare. I have reduced the framework to four principles that I would recommend to policy-makers as they work out the role of church-related welfare institutions in our society. These principles are not detailed recommendations but broad policies which might serve as directives to government and to the churches in determining their welfare roles and the mutual relationship they wish to see maintained.

VOLUNTARY ACTION

The first policy concerns voluntary action: in a democracy, government through its legislation should assure the total society of a strong voluntary welfare structure.

Government welfare seems to be the most universally efficient system of welfare services. Voluntary welfare is universally less efficient because it is restrictive and functions in a multiplicity of uncoordinated organizational units. Thus it happens that in the name of administrative efficiency there are put forth arguments for reducing all welfare to a common pattern and structure. These arguments are based on the size of modern society and its need for organizational efficiency and point to the need for greater government responsibility.

They are valid arguments carrying full pragmatic force and deserve a hearing: welfare programs and services must be more efficiently planned, coordinated, and organized; and government cannot avoid the responsibility that is incumbent on it for providing for the common welfare. Valid as they are, however, these arguments are frequently oversimplifications that obscure other values. Prior to all considerations of organizational efficiency is the principle that the human person is the subject of human values and that the administrative machinery that government constructs to serve him must be geared to the nature of the person who is to be served. The society that is conceived and organized as a mere machine comes into conflict with the human qualities of men that cannot be mechanized.

Things that can be expressed in quantity or reduced to calculable terms are easily collectivized: screws and bolts, water and electricity. Many other things are per se resistant to organization. Those things closest to the human spirit, the intangible, the incalculable, the élan of the human personality, defy collectivism. Peyser reflects the experience of all who have attempted to help another with an intimate human problem: "One cannot organize love and mothering, personal contact and interest. . . . Soup kitchens can be organized, moral rehabilitation cannot." [1]

Thus, society needs a principle to balance the principle of organization. Over a century ago Tocqueville spoke with what seems to have been prophetic warning of the need for voluntary action as the instrument to control the society's tendency toward depersonalization and absolutism. As society grows, he said, "the task of the governing power will . . . perpetually increase"; and the more it

[1] Peyser, *The Strong and the Weak*, p. 69.

increases, "the more will individuals, losing the notion of combining together, require its assistance." [2] Thus, the dialectic will proceed: government replaces free associations; individuals, losing the habit and will to cooperate voluntarily, turn to government for assistance; government responds and replaces free associations.

In our own century another French critic foresaw the American citizen caught up in an onrush toward efficiency and productivity "without giving a passing thought to the effect on his personality." [3] Writing about the American family, Siegfried saw a partial fulfillment of Tocqueville's evaluation: "In the eyes of the apostles of efficiency, the family is regarded as a barrier impeding the current." [4] Therefore, one function after another has passed from the family to other, less personal, and in some instances depersonalizing institutions. Like the family, other institutions are sometimes regarded as barriers to economic and administrative efficiency. In the search for instantaneous tangible results, the principle of pragmatism is invoked and the assembly-line technique is applied, sometimes to the detriment of the human person.

It is not a question of government or voluntary welfare, government versus voluntary welfare, as the problem was frequently stated in the 1930s. Every social means, if rightly used, can be an instrument for good. The problem is the right use of both government and voluntary welfare, and this requires a public policy that will assure government responsibility where necessary and a sister policy that will counterbalance government responsibility.

Modern governments must be endowed with the instruments for planning and the authority to assure unified action toward agreed-upon goals. Surely, even in a democracy, there are social mechanisms that if left uncontrolled corrupt a democracy from within. While it may be true that democracy itself is the surest counterbalance to these mechanisms, nevertheless, even a democratic society must plan the controls it will use, or things will end either in anarchy or in tyrannical absolutes. Speaking of the future of democratic societies, Mannheim says that they "will be ruled either by a minority in terms of a dictatorship or by a new form of gov-

[2] Tocqueville, *Democracy in America*, II, 116.
[3] Siegfried, *America Comes of Age*, p. 351.   [4] *Ibid.*

ernment which, in spite of its increased power will still be democratically controlled." [5]

Lord Beveridge recognized the need for this balance and the obligation that rests on government to assure it. Writing a decade after England had accepted his famed report, the father of the British welfare state issued a warning to democracies bent on the construction of welfare states:

> It is clear that the state must in the future do more things than it has attempted in the past. But it is equally clear, or should be equally clear, that room, opportunity, and encouragement must be kept for Voluntary Action in seeking new ways of social advance. There is need for political invention to find new ways of fruitful cooperation between public authorities and voluntary agencies. [6]

This is a repudiation of any simple and single panacea for the social problems of modern, complex society. History is full of charlatans who have made an easy living off the simple-minded who want a single rule-of-thumb solution to the world's problems. Social philosophies that attempt to organize society according to a single, one-sided, absolute concept are doomed to failure. No human problem can be met by a single solution. It is this desire for simple answers that fall neatly into manageable categories that leads disciples to compress and oversimplify and distort the teachings of their masters. Hardly is an innovator dead when well-intentioned followers inflate a sound segment of a system into a whole system, a process into an objective, a means into a philosophy of life. Having set England upon her course of state-welfarism and noted the trends in public policy, Beveridge thought it well to caution young enthusiasts:

> The State is or can be master of money, but in a free society it is master of very little else. The making of a good society depends not on the State but on the citizens, acting individually or in free association with one another, acting on motives of various kinds, some selfish others unselfish, some narrow and material, others inspired by love of God and love of man. The happiness or unhappiness of the society in which we live depends upon ourselves as citizens, not on the instrument of political power which we call the State. [7]

[5] Mannheim, *Diagnosis of Our Time*, p. 1.
[6] Beveridge, *Voluntary Action*, p. 10.   [7] *Ibid.*, p. 320.

Perhaps few statesmen can appreciate as could Beveridge the need for a comprehensive welfare plan in a modern democracy. Even fewer can appreciate that the state must meet this need by building voluntary action into its social structure. "The inevitable development of State action," Beveridge wrote, is a reality of modern democratic societies; for this very reason voluntary associations must be fostered by legislation, and governments must find "new forms which cooperation between the State and voluntary organizations may take." [8]

It would seem that the United States could benefit from Beveridge's recommendation for Great Britain, that the state encourage voluntary welfare and the cooperation of such groups with the state. The state cannot leave it to chance that voluntary welfare agencies will somehow find their place and carry out their responsibilities. The authority and power of government should be used in a positive way to assure the total society that voluntary agencies do assume this responsibility. A nation that is convinced of the value of citizen self-determination will so design public policies on the Federal, state, and local levels that government agencies will be enabled to use and strengthen voluntary services where they exist, assist in their initiation where they do not exist, and supply government services directly where they are needed.

WELFARE ROLE OF THE CHURCHES

The second principle concerns the welfare role of the churches: both for theological and sociological reasons the churches should carry a permanent social welfare responsibility that goes beyond pioneering and experimentation.

It is generally accepted that at least one predominant motive underlying church-related welfare is charity, whereas the predominant motive underlying government welfare programs is social justice. Unfortunately, some of its enthusiasts transform social justice into an ultimate value upon which alone they attempt to rest the social order. Then it happens that in the name of justice, charitable institutions are booked as hindrances. Either they are said not to be

[8] *Ibid.*, p. 10.

based on equality, the assumption being that in charitable institutions people of a superior status give to those of an inferior status and that this situation is undemocratic; [9] or the motive of charitable institutions is suspect, as, for example, it is said that "the love of man can often be degrading to all concerned." [10] In this way even charity may be considered an obstacle to social justice, and the recommendation is made that modern society "should strive toward that end where there will be no more charity." [11]

Every realist today will grant that an improved welfare structure will improve the level of social justice. But the "just society" needs more than social and economic justice, which are prey—as are the social and economic systems themselves—to moral or ethical imperfection and can become thereby social and economic injustice. As Mosca says, there is more to social justice than social structure:

No social organization can be based exclusively upon the sentiment of justice, and no social organization will ever fail to leave much to be desired from the standpoint of absolute justice. It is natural that things should be that way. In his private and public conduct no individual is ever guided exclusively by his sense of justice. He is guided by his passions and his needs. . . . The man of action, in political life or in business life, whether he be merchant or property owner, professional worker or laborer, priest of God or apostle of socialism, always tries to be a success, and his conduct, therefore, will always be a compromise, witting or unwitting, between his sense of justice and his interests.[12]

And Beveridge, while allowing that the responsibility of the state is to assure a just social order, recognizes nevertheless the limits of the state in achieving this objective. His words, "The State is or can be master of money, but in a free society it is master of very little else," [13] are a warning to men who would ground the social order on justice alone, forgetting that man's emotions, his love for others

[9] See Bourdillon, ed., *Voluntary Social Services*, p. 303.
[10] Arthur L. Swift, Jr., "The Church and Human Welfare," in F. Ernest Johnson, ed., *Religion and Social Work*, p. 12.
[11] Leo Pfeffer, "Commentary on Church and State Relations in Social Welfare," in Methodist Church, *Research Consultation on the Church and State*, Third Assembly, Chap. IV, p. 24.
[12] Mosca, *The Ruling Class*, pp. 287–88.
[13] Beveridge, *Voluntary Action*, p. 320, quoted previously.

as well as his self-interest, cannot be entirely divorced from his sense of justice.

But the "just society," even could it be realized socially and economically, would still leave men desiring something more than the mere justice provided by the system. For several reasons man wants from the social order more than social justice. As an individual person, man is not content with justice but has an innate desire to be valued as something more than an economic unit or a social or political category. This valuation must come to the citizen primarily from individual and family relationships of trust and love, but it must be reflected back to him also from the larger social patterns among which he finds his associations.

Institutions of justice, like the state, are by their very nature limited springs for these delicate values. They must come from outside the institutions of justice. Peyser suggests that the student compare the attitude of the state with the attitude of the church toward social problems, prostitution, for example. Since the virtue proper to the state is social justice, the attitude of the state is one of punishment, prohibition, and the control of economic and health factors and of antisocial behavior. These factors, if uncontrolled, "would be a . . . serious disturbance of public order, and, therefore, the State has to take certain measures." [14] The attitude of the church, on the other hand, embraces not only social justice but charity— physical, emotional, and moral rehabilitation. Theodore Maynard was probably not far from the mark when he said that a system based on social justice only and carrying the necessary social controls is something "the poor so very *rightly* loathe" [15] because it slights psychological, emotional, and spiritual needs.

Man wants more from the social order than justice for another reason: his desire to see the social order hold up to him his best self. He wants to have grounded in the social structure a value-ideal that will demand from him both a personal dedication based

---

[14] Peyser, *The Strong and the Weak*, p. 74.

[15] Catherine Lee Wahlstrom, "Religion and the Aged," in F. Ernest Johnson, ed., *Religion and Social Work*, pp. 113–14, quoting Theodore Maynard, *Apostle of Charity: the Life of St. Vincent de Paul*.

on conscience and a cooperation with all the other members of society toward the integration of this value-ideal. Only when the ideal is given a social form does it place on the members of society social obligations whose fulfilling welds human beings into a meaningful unity.[16] Something in the human person demands that society have such a unity, and this unity is beyond the reaches of social justice. On the source of this value-ideal and man's need for it, Mannheim says: "Certain unchanging aspects of the human mind seem to indicate the need for a transcendental religious foundation in society; and certain factors make this need even more urgent in our present situation."[17] Without this transcendental religious foundation society cannot lay claim to man's best and highest potential or answer his most important needs.

Man wants a social order that fulfills his psychological, social, and spiritual needs as well as his material wants. Those whose argument runs, "Give the people social security, food, shelter, and jobs, and all these problems will disappear," fail to understand the real social insecurity. They "do not realize that economic and social insecurity are only part of the general insecurity. They overlook the fact that psychological and spiritual insecurity are sometimes even more disturbing than the former."[18] Of what good is even the best welfare program if it is not concerned with man's deepest insecurity? Of what value are skillful methods and new techniques if we do not know what they are for and their relationship to the total person?[19]

The state can propose no more than a humanitarian ideal; it is beyond its scope and power to endow the social structure with a value-ideal based on conscience and grounded in a transcendental religious foundation. To achieve this end the state looks to society's value-ideal institutions, whose function it is to propose and implement such an ideal.

In a pluralistic society that ideal must necessarily have various facets. Therefore in a pluralistic society good social services, like good government, must be based on the principle of pluralism.

[16] Mannheim, *Systematic Sociology*, p. 126.
[17] Mannheim, *Freedom, Power and Democratic Planning*, pp. 288–89.
[18] *Ibid.*, p. 301.   [19] Mannheim, *Diagnosis of Our Time*, pp. 28–29.

They must be pluralistic in source, in method, in objective. They must be geared to the fulfillment of physical, emotional, and spiritual needs and must meet these needs on an individualized and personalized basis. For the achievement of many of the objectives of these services, the state can offer money and technical assistance. To meet psychological and spiritual insecurity, the state must ask the assistance of voluntary agencies and value-ideal institutions. Because these institutions spring into being out of man's deepest need, the state must strengthen them, for when they fade, the social order fails, and when they prosper, the social order gives promise of fulfilling man's deeper hopes.

Thus, for both religious and societal reasons, the responsibility for social welfare falls in part directly on the church: for religious reasons because the church has responsibility from God for the individual, for societal reasons because the church has responsibility also for the social order, to see that it is an amenable order in which the individual with the help of God may work out his perfection. This responsibility in the field of welfare cannot be carried out by "token gestures" at welfare by which the church merely salves its conscience. In a welfare society it must be carried out by a full-scale welfare program of the highest quality: otherwise it will fail—its own inadequacy will be its undoing—and it must be carried out directly by the churches; otherwise these programs will drift from their value base and fail to give the value-ideal that society rightly expects from the churches.

COOPERATION OF THE CHURCHES AND THE STATE

That society needs value-ideal institutions prepared to assume responsibility for the social order indicates the necessity of a third principle which concerns the relation of church and state: government and church-related welfare agencies should cooperate in the total welfare effort.

In many respects the churches have failed in their social responsibility. Two socio-religious principles—religious pluralism and a rigid interpretation of church-state separation—have weakened the churches' influence on society and brought about an exclusion of the churches from an active role in social policy. Mead thinks that our history as a nation under these two principles has now brought us full circle from the religious society of the Founding Fathers. Desiring to safeguard religious freedom, they laid down the principle of church-state separation. Encouraged by religious pluralism, the principle of separating church from state became a principle of separating church from society. The separation of church from society encouraged indifference to religion. Indifference to religion bred a religion of secularism which tends to be identified with American democratic society as a whole.

Through this chain of causes, the church in many quarters is no more influential in American life than other social or fraternal institutions that are formed by that life rather than being contributors to its formation. Thus the churches today are awakening to a realization that they are "entangled in a more subtle form of identification of Christianity, nationalism, and economic system than Christendom had ever known before." [20] As expressed by Philip Phenix, a former professor of philosophy at Columbia University,

It seems unfortunately to be the case that what has been presented as a means for preserving religious peace and freedom through secularization has to some extent become a method of propagating a particular dogmatic faith, namely, scientific naturalism or, to give it another name, naturalistic humanism.[21]

Sensing their declining influence, the churches have usually reacted by accommodating themselves to society and by reflecting society's values rather than by infusing society with religious values. In short, the churches abdicate their religious function in the interest of secular power. Thus the social control function proper to the churches is surrendered to political, social, and economic institutions. This abdication has tended to make the churches irrelevant as social institutions. Therefore church leaders are anxious to reconsider not only the social role of the churches but also the related question, the relationship of the churches to the state.

[20] Mead, "American Protestantism since the Civil War," *Journal of Religion*, XXXVI, No. 2 (April, 1956), 67.
[21] Phenix, "Religion in American Public Education," *Teachers College Record*, LVII, No. 1 (October, 1955), 30.

A reevaluation of that relationship in its total societal context is convincing many churchmen that cooperation of church and state is to their mutual advantage and so is for the good of the total society. The present social order seems to indicate that separation as historically understood, is no longer a viable principle and will have to give way in modern democracy to a principle of distinction and cooperation—distinction between the churches and the state and cooperation of the churches and the state. Even the ultraconservative organization, Protestants and Other Americans United for Separation of Church and State, which formerly spoke of church-state relationships in terms of "absolute separation," now speaks of a "friendly church-state separation."[22] Right-wing Protestantism, very similar in social policy to Catholicism, has in recent years proposed cooperation between the churches and the state not only in welfare but in other areas—as for example, education—which they formerly recognized as areas of separation.

The 1962 decision of the U.S. Supreme Court concerning the public school prayer of the New York Board of Regents was based on the fact that in our society no state official is a high priest and no governing body is a council of churchmen with the right to compose an obligatory prayer for public school children. This responsibility and this office fall outside the function of the state. Responsibilities of this nature belong to other social institutions, the role of the state being to allow for their accomplishment through these other institutions. The Supreme Court decision shocked many Americans to the point of questioning a church-state principle of absolute separation which is interpreted as noncooperation of church and state and caused them to suspect that the City of God and the City of Man must cooperate if the good society is to survive at all.

Perhaps that Supreme Court decision was the turning at the bend in the road. Perhaps the light beyond the bend will now point out more clearly the full implications of the principles our society has accepted all along: religion is the province of the church, religious-sponsored educational and welfare programs belong to the church, and our society will reflect a socio-religious ideal through a variety of educational and welfare programs—public and private, sectarian

[22] Lowell, *Separation and Religion*, p. 286.

and nonsectarian—only with the encouragement and support of the state. This pattern of partnership for a democratic, pluralistic society is based on a religious ideal.

As a church-state principle, noncooperation is no longer serviceable because all the institutions in modern society are so closely intertwined. The state and these institutions live in a kind of social symbiosis.[23] From the state flows a life and a power that determine what the other institutions of society shall be, and from the other institutions flow creative ideas and ideals that determine what the state shall be and what attitudes it shall adopt toward its citizens. That life flows both ways-between church and state is to the advantage of both. It is an advantage to the churches because it allows them to help construct a social order based upon man's transcendental aspirations; it is an advantage to the state because it allows the state to provide not only economic and social security but psychological and spiritual security as well.

In the matter of this cooperation between church and state, however, the churches must have a care for their motives—not to seek political advantage nor arrogate to themselves means of social control proper to the state. Similar care should be exercised by the state —not to seek the churches' approval and sanction in return for temporal favors. In this relationship of church and state, it is not the church that should seek the assistance of the state but rather the state that for its own temporal good should ask the assistance of the churches.[24] If we understand their right order, we know that, rather than the City of God seeking the assistance of the City of Man, it is more apt for the City of Man to ask the help of the City of God.[25] This order of assistance Mannheim had in mind when he stated that it is simply sound politics for the state to be aware of and provide for more than the economic and social security of a people.[26]

For the greater good of society, the state should ask a greater contribution of church-related welfare associations. Without arbitrary preference but on the basis of the equality of all citizens, the state should ask the cooperation of the churches in all activities that

---

[23] Peyser, *The Strong and the Weak*, p. 87.
[24] Maritain, *Man and the State*, p. 179.   [25] *Ibid.*, p. 178.
[26] Mannheim, *Freedom, Power and Democratic Planning*, p. 301.

nourish and strengthen the personal and social value-ideal. In order to fulfill their social responsibility, the churches must work cooperatively with government at the same time that they maintain their distinction and autonomy. Speaking from his own experience and from all Europe's tragedy, Maritain gives his formula for church and state in a pluralistic society: "Sharp distinction *and* actual cooperation, that's a historical treasure, the value of which a European is perhaps more prepared to appreciate, because of his own bitter experience." [27]

A decision to follow a policy of church-state cooperation in welfare involves for the churches two further related policy decisions. First, welfare executives need to establish limits of financial dependency on tax funds. Although construction grants and purchase of service in some areas of welfare seem sound methods of encouraging voluntary responsibility, no voluntary agency should become so totally dependent on tax support that it is nothing more than a funnel for government money and policies. It is difficult to determine limits for agencies in all regions of the nation and under all circumstances, but one could question the autonomy of an agency that receives much more than 50 percent of its operating budget from tax sources. Responsibility for thinking through these policies belongs to church welfare executives. Unless they indicate to their local agency administrators church-state principles that are both clear and realistic for today's society, the policies of the sectarian agencies will continue to grow haphazardly, completely eluding the guidance and ideal of the churches.

Second, voluntary welfare must recognize its responsibility to the total community. In an aristocratic society responsibility is concentrated at one point, in an individual or select group, while individual responsibility is minimal. In democratic societies social responsibility is diffused throughout the individuals and the institutions that make up the social system. In a less structured, more laissez-faire society, voluntary associations were truly "private" and could go their own way without greatly affecting the total welfare system. This is no longer true.

The once private character of voluntary welfare has changed. Almost overnight the political system has been transformed into a

[27] Maritain, *Man and the State*, p. 183.

social welfare system, of which voluntary welfare is a part. If it intends to demand a significant role in the system, it must accept its responsibility to plan for total community needs. If voluntary welfare endorses a policy of partnership whereby it enjoys the advantages of the tax power of the state, it must acknowledge its obligation of public accountability and responsibility to the entire community. Voluntary welfare agencies can no longer operate on policies that governed their programs thirty or forty years ago. Thirty or forty years ago they were truly private. At their founding they were sponsored by small interest groups, served a small clientele, and were financed by private appeals for funds from certain closed groups.

Today the originating spirit behind a voluntary health or welfare service may still be a select group of persons related to a church or to some philanthropic association, but on its board of directors sit Protestants, Catholics, and Jews as well as civic leaders of no particular religious conviction. Its appeal for funds goes far beyond the church doors or the walls of a private organization. In most cases it asks that the community as a whole recognize its responsibility to finance the voluntary service, and in most cases some of its budget is from tax funds. Such an agency is still voluntary, but it is no longer private. Although administratively it belongs to a private group, that group exists and depends for its existence upon hundreds of other institutions in the community. Such an agency carries responsibility and accountability to that community.

These minor policy decisions must be faced by voluntary welfare organizations. With one eye to their voluntary character and the other eye to their community responsibility, they must determine both the degree to which they want to become dependent on tax funds and the extent of their willingness to be accountable to the community at large.

ECUMENICALISM IN SOCIAL WELFARE

The fourth principle concerns the cooperation among the churches in the field of welfare: the welfare departments of the churches should collaborate in forming and effecting social policy.

The foregoing study has singled out efforts at collaboration among the churches. Protestant, Catholic, and Jewish welfare leaders have already identified a unity of purpose in their welfare programs. Furthermore, although a surface view might not indicate it, a more prolonged look shows that many of the churches already have a certain unity in social philosophy. Much of the apparent discord arises from poor communication and from language barriers. At the top level, where Protestants, Catholics, and Jews carry on a continuous dialogue on social policy, the communications barrier is being broken and national leaders of different churches are finding that in many instances they think alike. The different conceptions that the churches have of their role in society are presently coming closer together; the prospect is that in time they will form a single view.

Similar meetings by Protestant, Catholic, and Jewish welfare executives should be encouraged on the local level. This is necessary for two reasons. First, church welfare policies, as we have seen in many instances, are determined at the level of the local agency. Second, also at the local level government administrators frequently make significant policy decisions that affect voluntary welfare. Therefore, social policy dialogue and formation on the local level should not only include church welfare executives, but should also include local government administrators. Every community should provide a more stable structure through which government and voluntary welfare executives, sectarian and nonsectarian, may plan together to meet welfare needs.

It is clear from the analysis in Chapter 3 that the churches have various role conceptions of themselves both as religious and social institutions. It is also clear that the differences in social role stem at least partially from theological differences between the churches. Ultimately these differences have their origins in the nature of the church as understood by the various religious groups. These theological differences are real and are rooted in differing interpretations of revelation. Moreover, as a result of the action of history they have acquired a certain crystallization that does not render them amenable to solution.

Fortunately, however, history itself is showing signs of dissolving the differences that separate the churches, immediately not so much through direct theological dialogue as through dialogue in the fields of education, politics, community action, and social problems. These are more fundamental levels of unity and ecumenicalism where men must conceive and achieve a common personal and social ideal before they can arrive at a common theological ideal. Theological ecumenicalism needs a base in human society, an accepted social ideal upon which to rest. Divine grace does not abrogate individual nature but builds upon it and perfects it; likewise, the church does not sweep a society aside but grows out of it and perfects it. The mending of the rent in the church will be hastened, perhaps it will be possible, only by fusing into a harmony the disparate elements in our society that keep us from achieving a common individual and social ideal. Social policy is one level where churchmen and laymen meet in an effort at elaborating this ideal. It is a level of practical and theoretical importance where the ground can be prepared for a richer ecumenicalism.

Church welfare executives have no reason to fear this form of ecumenicalism. Rather is the reverse true: they have cause for concern as long as they continue to emphasize their diversities. Where religious leaders stress conflicting social philosophies and value-ideals that clash, they retard social unity and promote the value distintegration of society. Religious leaders are well aware of the doctrinal matters that separate one religion from another, nor is the purpose of ecumenicalism in social welfare to dissolve doctrinal differences. But different theological positions can and frequently do sustain a common social policy, and today many areas of social philosophy and public policy do not pertain directly to theology.

The churches are rightly concerned about social policy issues and should lend their united strength toward identifying a common social philosophy and effecting a common social policy. The ecumenical spirit itself is a reflection of the awareness of the churches that a heavy responsibility lies upon them to achieve at least these intermediate goals, to dissolve barriers of divisiveness and to unite in forming a social order that will have at its center the best of the Judeo-Christian character.

Unity in these areas of public life is a twofold gain: it is an advance toward a social unity that every society needs, and it can be an advance toward the goal of doctrinal ecumenicalism. Ecumenicalism in social policy formation can be a gateway to religious ecumenicalism. For this reason religious leaders who are interested in the ecumenical movement look with favor and hope on the collaboration of the churches in social welfare and social action. This form of unity is one strand in the unity of thought and spirit that one day hopefully will unite the churches.

APPENDIX I. RESPONSE TO QUESTIONNAIRE

TABLE A1. *Number of Questionnaires Sent and Returned,*
by Denomination

Denomination	Number Sent	Number Returned	Other[a]
Nonsectarian	223[b]	85	10
Jewish	101	63	4
Catholic	352	107	29
Protestant	409	152	49
American Baptist	36	8	8
Southern Baptist	37	12	3
Episcopal	87	26	13
Evangelical and Reformed	29	10	3
Lutheran	122	48	14
Methodist	98	42	8
Other	...	6[b]	...
Total	1,085	407	92

[a] Includes questionnaires that could not be used in the study because the agencies no longer existed or because the information given was insufficient.

[b] When six of the questionnaires sent under the assumption that the agencies were nonsectarian were returned, the administrators indicated that the agencies were Protestant but did not state the specific denomination.

TABLE A2. Response to Questionnaire, by Type of Service and Denomination

Response	Nonsectarian	Jewish	Catholic	Protestant	Total
Hospitals:					
Returned	23	9	12	36	80
Not returned	25	10	35	71	141
Total	48	19	47	107	221
Homes for the aged:					
Returned	15	20	12	56	103
Not returned	33	14	65	101	213
Total	48	34	77	157	316
Children's services:					
Returned	47	34	83	60	224
Not returned	70	10	116	36	232
Total	117	44	199	96	456

APPENDIX II. AGENCIES
RECEIVING TAX FUNDS

Table A3 shows the large percentage of voluntary agencies that receive tax funds either by way of subsidy or purchase of service.

TABLE A3. *Number of Agencies Receiving and Not Receiving Funds, by Affiliation*

Affiliation	Total	Receiving Funds	Not Receiving Funds
Nonsectarian	85	62	23
Jewish	63	41	22
Catholic	107	89	18
Protestant	152	98	54
American Baptist	8	4	4
Southern Baptist	12	3	9
Episcopal	26	19	7
Evangelical and Reformed	10	6	4
Lutheran	48	37	11
Methodist	42	23	19
Other Protestant[a]	6	6	...
Total	407	290	117

[a] Questionnaire sent under the assumption that the agency was nonsectarian and returned with the information that it was Protestant, although specific denomination was not given.

Table A4 shows the willingness of the agencies that do receive tax funds to disclose the extent and nature of the tax support they receive by submitting for the purposes of this study a financial statement. Here, as elsewhere in this study, there was wide variation in the cooperation of Protestant denominations. Episcopal agencies were remarkably co-operative, all but one handing in a statement of budget; Lutherans were almost as cooperative, about three-fourths of their agencies making known their budgets. Methodist, Baptist, and Evangelical and Reformed agencies were conspicuously protective about their fiscal affairs.

TABLE A4. *Number of Agencies That Receive Tax Funds and That Submitted Full Financial Statements, by Affiliation*

Affiliation	Receive Tax Funds	Full Financial Statement
Nonsectarian	62	47
Jewish	41	39
Catholic	89	73
Protestant	98	68
American Baptist	4	1
Southern Baptist	3	1
Episcopal	19	18
Evangelical and Reformed	6	3
Lutheran	37	28
Methodist	23	13
Other Protestant [a]	6	4
Total	290	227

[a] Questionnaire sent under the assumption that the agency was nonsectarian and returned with the information that it was Protestant, although specific denomination was not given.

APPENDIX III. DIFFERENCES IN AGENCIES BY TYPE OF SERVICE

SIZE OF AGENCIES

The size of an agency is usually expressed in terms of its budget. By this yardstick the welfare institutions in this study—children's services, homes for the aged, and children's institutions—are remarkably similar in size. The fiscal operations of the three types of services are distributed into three categories: small, annual budget of less than $100,000; medium, annual budget between $100,000 and $200,000; large, annual budget of $200,000 and over. Table A5 shows that voluntary children's services tend to have larger fiscal programs. Homes for the aged are smaller than children's services and somewhat larger than children's institutions. None of these homes has a budget of over $1,000,000. Although children's institutions are the smallest of the three services, in this category are found the greatest variation in kind and the widest range in size. Many of these institutions are orphanages, but some are well-staffed residential treatment centers; four institutions for children, for example, have budgets of between $500,000 and $1,000,000, and one spends more than $1,000,000 annually.

TABLE A5. Size of Budgets, by Type of Service

Type of Service	Size of Program			Total	
	Small[a]	Medium[b]	Large[c]	No.	%
Children's services	14	23	23	60	32
Homes for the aged	10	17	11	38	21
Children's institutions	32	28	26	86	47
Total	56	68	60	184	100

[a] Annual budget less than $100,000.
[b] Annual budget between $100,000 and $200,000.
[c] Annual budget $200,000 or greater.

SUPPORT BY TAX FUNDS

In terms of their total fiscal operation, hospitals receive the smallest proportion of government assistance toward their annual budgets. Of the 43 hospitals in the sample, 27 receive less than 10 percent of their budgets from tax funds; 35 receive less than 30 percent of income from government sources.

The pattern of tax-funds assistance for children's services follows rather closely the same pattern as that of the hospitals: 28 children's services receive from tax funds less than 10 percent of their total budgets, and 44 receive less than 30 percent. Proportionately, therefore, voluntary children's service programs are slightly more dependent on tax funds than are the hospitals in this study. Stated in terms of comparative self-support, a very large percentage of the agencies in these two welfare categories receive from government only a small proportion of their income (Figure 3).

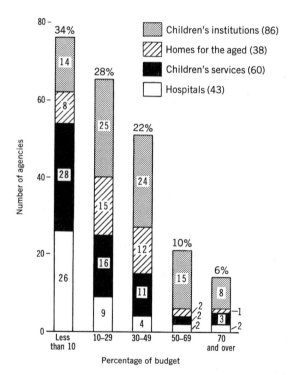

FIGURE 3. Percentage of tax funds in budgets of 227 agencies, by type of service.

The institutional programs for children and for the aged benefit noticeably more than do hospitals and children's services. Of 38 homes for the aged only 8 receive less than 10 percent of budget from tax funds; 15 receive from 10 to 29 percent of income; 12 receive from 30 to 49 percent.

Children's institutions receive more in tax funds than do children's services and homes for the aged. Only 14 receive less than 10 percent of budget from tax sources; 25 receive between 10 and 29 percent; 24 receive between 30 and 49 percent. Hence 23 of the 86 institutional programs for children depend upon government for more than one-half of their incomes.

TYPE OF PAYMENT

A voluntary institution may receive tax assistance in one of three general ways: subsidy is an annual lump-sum payment made to the institution by a governmental body; flat amounts per case per month are set per capita payments made to the voluntary institution for each case treated each month; percentage-of-cost payments are percentages per capita payments made to the voluntary institution for each case treated each month. In most instances where agencies receive from government both per-case and percentage-of-cost payment, this arrangement is necessary because the agency sells its services to two counties or to two government agencies in the same county that operate on different reimbursement policies.[1]

Of the 227 agencies receiving reimbursement from government funds, 155 receive flat amounts per case per month, 46 receive a certain percentage of service cost, and 26 receive per case both a flat amount and a percentage of cost. Of the 181 agencies that receive flat amounts only 149 stated clearly the amount received per case per month. These amounts range from less than $50 to more than $300. Although the larger amounts are generally paid to hospitals, there are included in this higher bracket some residential treatment centers for children.

Figure 4 gives a comparative picture of the flat amounts received per case per month by agencies in the four categories in this study. Children's service programs receive relatively small sums; two-thirds of these agencies receive from $50 to $75 per case per month. The greatest variation in the range of per case per month amounts—from less than $50 to more

[1] For a listing of state policies on types of payments to voluntary agencies for child welfare services, see Ruth M. Werner, *Public Financing of Voluntary Agency Foster Care* (Child Welfare League of America, Inc., New York 10, N.Y., 1961).

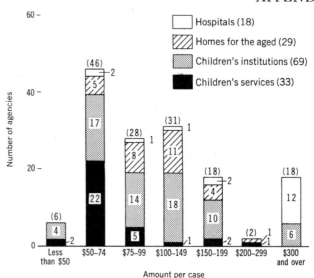

FIGURE 4. *Amount received for purchase of service per case, by type of service for 149 agencies.*

than $300—is found among children's institutions: about one-fourth of the institutions receiving from $50 to $74, one-fifth from $75 to $99, and one-fourth from $100 to $149. The variation in amounts corresponds to the variation in types of agencies, and the range reflects the kind and quality of service. What is also reflected by variation and range of per-case amounts is the tendency of some government agencies to purchase expensive treatment service rather than pay for mere custodial care. The per-case payments to nursing homes follow most closely the normal curve of distribution. This is understandable, since the needs of the aged in nursing homes are fairly constant. Although the total amounts received by hospitals from government constitute only a small percentage of their total costs, the hospital service per case is so costly that government reimbursement to hospitals is out on another curve altogether.

APPENDIX IV. DISTRIBUTION OF HILL-BURTON FUNDS

Table A6 shows the number of hospitals in the United States that have a sectarian affiliation and that had received funds for hospital construction under the Hill-Burton Act as of December 31, 1960. The table shows the percentage of Protestant, Catholic, and Jewish hospitals and the total amount of funds that they have received under the Act. The average amount of funds received per hospital is not the average grant but the average amount of money granted per hospital; many hospitals have received several, some as many as five or six, separate grants for different projects. The average amount received per Protestant hospital was considerably below the general average. The average amount received per Catholic hospital was somewhat above the general average. The average amount received per Jewish hospital, was below the general average but higher than the Protestant average. There are also differences in the amounts accounted for by the Protestant denominations.

It is clear that Protestant Hill-Burton hospitals tend to be concentrated in the rural regions, whereas Catholic Hill-Burton hospitals tend to be concentrated in the urban, industrial areas where the Catholic population is heaviest. The concentration of Protestant and Catholic hospitals that receive Hill-Burton grants is illustrated in Figure 5, the geographical division used being that followed by the Social Security Administration of the Department of Health, Education, and Welfare.

Table A7 shows the exact numbers of Protestant, Catholic, and Jewish hospitals receiving Hill-Burton grants and their geographical distribution as of December 31, 1960.

TABLE A6. Sectarian Hospitals Receiving Hill-Burton Funds, by Number and Amounts

Affiliation	Total		Receiving Hill-Burton Funds		Funds Received			Average per Hospital
	No.	%	No.	%	Amount	%		
Jewish	57	3.5	28	4.4	$ 14,588,744	4.4		$503,060
Catholic	889	55.3	370	58.4	202,775,912	61.5		552,522
Protestant	662	41.2	236	37.2	112,505,669	34.1		476,718
American Baptist	7	0.4	2	0.3	1,193,365	0.4		596,682
Southern Baptist	40	2.5	12	1.9	6,088,407	1.8		507,367
Episcopalian	49	3.1	19	3.0	10,615,186	3.2		558,694
Evangelical and Reformed	9	0.6	5	0.8	4,006,264	1.2		801,252
Lutheran	116	7.2	71	11.1	16,558,675	5.0		223,220
Methodist	76	4.7	46	7.3	32,301,949	9.8		702,216
Other Protestant	365	22.7	81	12.8	41,741,823	12.7		515,331
Total	1,608	100.0	634	100.0	$329,870,325	100.0		$520,300

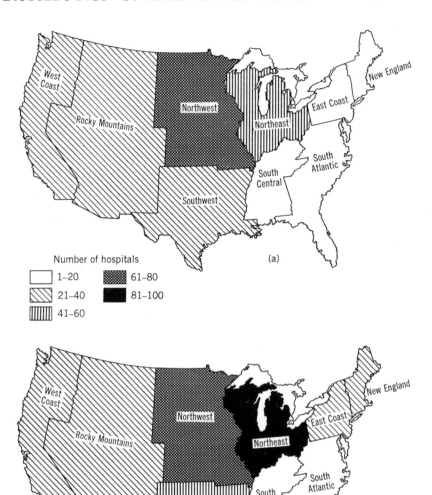

Number of hospitals (a)

☐	1–20	▨	61–80
▧	21–40	■	81–100
▥	41–60		

FIGURE 5. Geograpical distribution of hospitals that have received Hill-Burton grants: (a) 236 Protestant hospitals; (b) 370 Catholic hospitals.

*TABLE A7. Sectarian Hospitals Receiving Hill-Burton Grants,
by Geographical Region and Affiliation*

Region	Protestant		Catholic		Jewish, No.
	No.	%	No.	%	
New England	1	0.4	25	6.8	4
East Coast	10	4.2	33	8.9	7
South Atlantic	17	7.2	18	4.9	3
South Central	8	3.4	18	4.9	1
Southwest	27	11.4	42	11.3	1
Northeast	43	18.2	97	26.2	5
Northwest	71	30.1	76	20.5	2
Rocky Mountains	38	16.1	27	7.3	...
West Coast	21	9.0	34	9.2	5
Total	236	100.0	370	100.0	28

APPENDIX V. QUESTIONS ON POLICY

The following three questions were put to local administrators of voluntary welfare agencies in order to learn their attitudes on government assistance in relation to the principle of church-state separation and to agency autonomy. The more significant results are shown in Tables A8 to A12.

A. In your opinion does the payment of tax funds to sectarian health and social welfare agencies either as a lump-sum payment or as purchase of service constitute a violation of the American principle of separation of church and state? Please check the degree of violation, if any, which you consider exists. In the space below please comment.

Degree of Violation	Type of Payment	
	Subsidy	Purchase of Service
No violation		
Some violation but not sufficiently serious to cause doubt about sectarian health and welfare agencies' receiving public funds.		
Considerable violation, sufficient to make me doubt whether sectarian health and welfare agencies should receive tax funds.		
Extreme violation, so much so that I do not think sectarian health and welfare agencies should receive tax funds.		

B. In your opinion does the receipt of government funds either as a lump-sum payment or on basis of purchase of service by a private sectarian health or welfare agency conflict with the principles or ideology of your agency? Please check the degree of conflict, if any, which you consider exists. In the space below, please comment.

Degree of Conflict	Type of Payment	
	Subsidy	Purchase of Service
No conflict; no reason for concern over receipt of tax funds.		
Some conflict but not sufficient to cause doubt as to the policy of accepting tax funds.		
Considerable conflict; enough to cause doubt that sectarian agencies should receive tax funds.		
Extreme conflict; sufficient concern to make me think that sectarian agencies should not receive tax funds.		

C. Setting aside your agency's principles or ideology and setting aside the principle of separation of church and state, in your opinion are there any dangers to voluntary health and welfare agencies (whether sectarian or non-sectarian) in accepting tax funds for their service programs? Please check the degree of danger, if any, which you consider exists. In the space below, please comment.

Degree of Danger	Type of Payment	
	Subsidy	Purchase of Service
No danger.		
Some danger, but not sufficient to cause doubt about receiving tax funds.		
Considerable danger, sufficient to cause doubt about receiving tax funds.		
Extreme danger, so much so that I do not think agencies should receive tax funds.		

TABLE A8. Number of Agencies Giving Opinion as to Degree That Subsidy Violates Principle of Church-State Separation, by Affiliation

Degree of Violation	Total No.	%	Protestant	Catholic	Jewish	Nonsectarian
None	112	44	23	50	23	16
Some [a]	49	20	17	4	15	13
Considerable [b]	41	16	23	4	5	9
Extreme [c]	50	20	35	...	2	13
Total	252 [d]	100	98	58	45	51

[a] But no doubt about accepting funds.
[b] Enough to cause doubt about accepting funds.
[c] Funds should not be accepted
[d] Of the 407 participants in the study, 13 were uncertain and 142 did not respond to the question.

TABLE A9. Number of Agencies Giving Opinion as to Degree That Subsidy Endangers Agency Autonomy, by Affiliation

Degree of Danger	Total No.	%	Protestant	Catholic	Jewish	Nonsectarian
None	76	29	18	21	20	17
Some [a]	70	26	19	19	18	14
Considerable [b]	71	27	31	20	7	13
Extreme [c]	47	18	36	3	...	8
Total	264 [d]	100	104	63	45	52

[a] But no doubt about accepting funds.
[b] Enough to cause doubt about accepting funds.
[c] Funds should not be accepted.
[d] Of the 407 participants in the study, 6 were uncertain and 137 did not respond to the question.

TABLE A10. Number of Agencies Giving Opinion as to Degree That Purchase of Service Violates Principle of Church-State Separation, by Affiliation

Degree of Violation	Total No.	%	Protestant	Catholic	Jewish	Nonsectarian
None	265	76	82	90	47	46
Some [a]	46	13	29	1	9	7
Considerable [b]	17	5	11	...	2	4
Extreme [c]	21	6	14	...	...	7
Total	349 [d]	100	136	91	58	64

[a] But no doubt about accepting funds.
[b] Enough to cause doubt about accepting funds.
[c] Funds should not be accepted.
[d] Of the 407 participants in the study, 6 were uncertain and 52 did not respond to the question.

TABLE A11. *Number of Agencies Giving Opinion as to Degree That Purchase of Service Endangers Agency Autonomy, by Affiliation*

Degree of Danger	Total No.	Total %	Protestant	Catholic	Jewish	Nonsectarian
None	195	55	64	54	41	36
Some [a]	105	30	40	30	13	22
Considerable [b]	36	10	18	8	4	6
Extreme [c]	18	5	15	...	...	3
Total	354 [d]	100	137	92	58	67

[a] But no doubt about accepting funds.

[b] Enough to cause doubt about accepting funds.

[c] Funds should not be accepted.

[d] Of the 407 participants in the study, 5 were uncertain and 48 did not respond to the question.

TABLE A12. *Protestant Attitude toward Purchase of Service as a Violation of Church-State Separation, by Denomination*

Denomination	Positive Response [a]	Negative Response [b]	Total
Lutheran	37	5	42
Methodist	33	6	39
Episcopal	21	1	22
Evangelical and Reformed	6	3	9
American Baptist	5	2	7
Southern Baptist	4	8	12
Other Protestant [c]	5	...	5
Total	111	25	136

[a] No violation at all or negligible violation.

[b] Considerable or extreme violation.

[c] Responses to questionnaires sent under the assumption that the agency was nonsectarian and returned with the information that it was Protestant, although specific denomination was not given.

BIBLIOGRAPHY

PUBLISHED SOURCES

Abbott, Grace. *The Child and the State*. Chicago, University of Chicago Press, 1938. Vol. II.

American Jewish Committee. *American Jewish Yearbook 1956, 1958*. Philadelphia, Jewish Publication Society, 1956, 1958. Vols. LVII, LVIX.

American Jewish Congress. "Religious Freedom in the United States," *Congress Weekly*, XXII, No. 33 (November 28, 1955), 12–16 (statement of the American Jewish Congress on "Freedom of Religion and Separation of Church and State" submitted to the Subcommittee on Constitutional Rights of the U.S. Senate on the Judiciary).

American Lutheran Church, Board of Christian Social Action. *Aims and Purposes of the American Lutheran Church in Its Program for Christian Social Action*. The Board, n.d.

—— *The Christian and His Social Living* (compilation of study and discussion on social issues made by the Board of Christian Social Action). Minneapolis, the Board, 1960.

Andrews, F. Emerson. *Attitudes towards Giving*. New York, Russell Sage Foundation, 1953.

—— *Philanthropic Giving*. New York, Russell Sage Foundation, 1950.

Aronson, Arnold. "Organization of the Community Relations Field," *Journal of Intergroup Relations*, I, No. 2 (Spring, 1960), 18–32.

Bachmann, E. Theodore, ed. *The Activating Concern: Historical and Theological Bases*. Vol. I of "Churches and Social Welfare" series. New York, National Council of Churches, 1955.

—— *The Emerging Perspective: Response and Prospect* (proceedings of the First Conference on the Churches and Social Welfare). Vol. III of "Churches and Social Welfare" series. New York, National Council of Churches, 1956.

Bernstein, Philip. "Current and Prospective Trends in Jewish Communal Services," *Journal of Jewish Communal Service*, XXXV, No. 1 (Fall, 1958), 15–23.

Beveridge, William Henry [Lord Beveridge]. *Voluntary Action*. New York, Macmillan, 1948.

Blanshard, Paul. *The Bus Wedge*. Washington, D.C., Protestants and Other Americans United for Separation of Church and State, n.d.

——— *God and Man in Washington*. Boston, Beacon Press, 1960.

Blau, Peter M. *Bureaucracy in Modern Society*. New York, Random House, 1956.

Bogen, Boris D. *Jewish Philanthropy*. New York, Macmillan, 1917.

Bourdillon, A. F. C., ed. *Voluntary Social Services, Their Place in the Modern State*. London, Methuen, 1945.

Branscombe, Martha. "Basic Policies and Principles of Public Child Care Services: An Underlying Philosophy," *Child Welfare*, February, 1952 (special issue), pp. 2–9.

Brown, James, IV. "The Outlook for Private Philanthropy," *Child Welfare*, XXX, No. 3 (May, 1951), 11–12.

Burns, Eveline M. *Social Security and Public Policy*. New York, McGraw-Hill, 1956.

Butler, Msgr. John J. "Discussion: The Point of View of the Multiple Function Agency," *Child Welfare*, February, 1952 (special issue), pp. 12–14

Cayton, Horace R., and Setsuko Matsunaga Nishi, eds. *The Changing Scene: Current Trends and Issues*. Vol. II of "Churches and Social Welfare" series. New York, National Council of Churches, 1955.

Chakerian, Charles G., ed. *The Churches and Social Welfare*. Hartford, Conn., Hartford Seminary Foundation, 1955.

Clancy, William P., *et al. Catholicism in America* (a series of articles originally published in *Commonweal*). New York, Harcourt, Brace, 1953. See especially William P. Clancy, "Catholicism in America"; Will Herberg, "A Jew Looks at Catholics"; John J. Kane, "Catholic Separatism"; and Reinhold Niebuhr, "A Protestant Looks at Catholics."

Clark, Kenneth B. "Jews in Contemporary America," *Jewish Social Service Quarterly*, XXXI, No. 1 (Fall, 1954), 12–22.

Cohen, Nathan E., ed. *The Citizen Volunteer*. New York, Harper and Row, 1960.

Corson, John J. "Social Security and the Welfare State," *Social Service Review*, XXIV, No. 1 (March, 1950), 8–12.

Coughlin, Bernard J., s.j. "Private Welfare in a Public Welfare Bureaucracy," *Social Service Review*, XXXV, No. 2 (June, 1961), 184–93.

Crain, James A. *Christian Action and Community Service*. Indianapolis, Church Program Planning Committee of the Disciples of Christ, n.d.

Davies, Stanley P. "The Churches and the Non-Sectarian Agencies," *Better Times*, January 22, 1954. (Reprint published by the Health and Welfare Council of New York City.)

Dawson, Joseph Martin. *America's Way in Church, State, and Society.* New York, Macmillan, 1953.

Doebele, John. "Pius' Basic Social Address," *Social Order*, II, No. 9 (November, 1952), 397–403.

de Gracia, Alfred, ed. *Grass Roots Private Welfare.* New York, New York University Press, 1957.

Drucker, Peter F. *The New Society.* New York, Harper, 1950.

Eliot, Charles W. "The Exemption from Taxation of Church Property and the Property of Educational, Literary, and Charitable Institutions," in *American Contributions to Civilization*, 1898.

Fanfani, Amintore. *Catholicism, Protestantism and Capitalism.* New York, Sheed and Ward, 1955.

Faris, Laune, and Todd Faris, eds. *Intelligent Philanthropy.* Chicago, University of Chicago Press, 1930.

Federation of Jewish Philanthropies of New York. *To Serve the Children Best: A Community Program for Jewish Child Care.* New York, the Federation, 1956.

Finkelstein, Louis, ed. *The Jews: Their History, Culture, and Religion.* New York, Harper and Row, 1960.

Frankel, Emil. "Relationships between Public and Private Agencies for the Care of Dependent and Neglected Children," *Social Service Review*, VII (1933), 640–54.

Fromm, Erich. *Escape from Freedom.* New York, Rinehart, 1941.

Furfey, Paul Hanly. "The Churches and Social Problems," *Annals of the American Academy of Political and Social Science*, CCLVI (March, 1948), 101–09.

Garrison, Winfred E. "Characteristics of American Organized Religion," *Annals of the American Academy of Political and Social Science*, CCLVI (March, 1948), 14–24.

Gerth, Hans, and C. Wright Mills, eds. *From Max Weber, Essays in Sociology.* New York, Oxford University Press, 1958.

Gilbert, Arthur. "Religion and the Free Society," *Reconstructionist*, XXIV, No. 11 (October 3, 1958), 6–12.

Glock, Charles Y. "Issues That Divide: A Postscript," *Journal of Social Issues*, XII, No. 3 (1956), 40–43.

Glueck, Sheldon, ed. *The Welfare State and the National Welfare.* Cambridge, Mass., Addison-Wesley, 1952.

Goldstein, Sidney E. *The Synagogue and Social Welfare.* New York, Bloch, 1955.

Gordon, Andrew. *Security, Freedom and Happiness.* London, Catholic Social Guild, 1948.

Grants of Land and Gifts of Money to Catholic and Non-Catholic Institutions in New York Compared. New York, Catholic Publications Society, 1879.

Greene, Evarts B. *Church and State.* Indianapolis, National Foundation Press, 1947.

——— *Religion and the State.* New York, New York University Press, 1941.

Grossman, Mordecai. "A Civilization within a Civilization?" *Commentary,* I, No. 1 (November, 1945), 39–46.

Guilfoyle, Bishop George H. "Church-State Relations in Welfare," *Catholic Lawyer,* III, No. 2 (April, 1957), 112–28.

Hager, Don J. "Introduction: Religious Conflict," *Journal of Social Issues,* XII, No. 3 (1956), 3–11.

Harrison, Paul M. *Authority and Power in the Free Church Tradition.* Princeton, N.J., Princeton University Press, 1959.

Head, Rev. Edward D. *Principles of Cost Accounting for Church-Related Agencies Where Public or Community Funds Are Involved.* Mimeographed.

Herberg, Will. *Judaism and Modern Man: An Interpretation of Jewish Religion.* New York, Farrar, Straus, 1951. (Paperback edition, Meridian Books, 1959.)

——— *Protestant, Catholic, Jew: An Essay in American Religious Sociology.* New York, Doubleday, 1956.

Hofstadter, Richard. *Social Darwinism in American Thought.* Boston, Beacon Press, 1955.

Hutchinson, John A., ed. *Christian Faith and Social Action.* New York, Scribner's, 1953.

Jacobson, Philip. "Community Relations Implications in the Use of Public Funds by Jewish Services," *Journal of the Jewish Communal Services,* XXXVII, No. 1 (Fall, 1960), 112–18.

Jenkins, Edward C. *Philanthropy in America.* New York, Association Press, 1950.

Johnson, Arlien. *Public Policy and Private Charities.* Chicago, University of Chicago Press, 1931.

——— "The Respective Roles of Governmental and Voluntarily Supported Social Work," *Social Service Review,* XXII (1948), 298–311.

Johnson, F. Ernest. *The Church and Society.* New York, Abingdon-Cokesbury, 1935.

———, ed. *Religion and Social Work.* New York, Harper, 1956.

Judson, Edward. "The Church in Its Social Aspects," *Annals of the American Academy of Political and Social Science,* XXX, No. 3 (November, 1907), 1–12.

Kahn, Alfred J., ed. *Issues in American Social Work.* New York, Columbia University Press, 1959.

Kaplan, Mordecai M. "The Truth about Reconstructionism," *Commentary*, I, No. 2 (December, 1945), 50–59.

Kasius, Cora, ed. *New Directions in Social Work*. New York, Harper, 1954.

Kelley, Dean M. *Questions of Church and State*. New York, Board of Social and Economic Relations of the Methodist Church, 1960.

Kertzer, Morris M. "Religions in a Democratic Society," *Reconstructionist*, XXV, No. 1 (February 20, 1959), 6.

King, Wilfred Isabel. *Trends in Philanthropy*. New York, National Bureau of Economic Research, 1928.

Konvitz, Milton R. "Whittling Away Religious Freedom," *Commentary*, I, No. 8 (June, 1946), 4–13.

Kravitz, Jacob H. "Comment: What Price Public Funds?" *Journal of Jewish Communal Service*, XXXVII, No. 1 (Fall, 1960), 119–23.

Kurtz, Russell H., ed. *Social Work Year Book*. 12th edition, American Association of Social Workers, 1954. 13th edition, National Association of Social Workers, 1957. New York.

Kutzik, Alfred J. *Social Work and Jewish Values*. Washington, D.C., Public Affairs Press, 1959.

Leo XIII. "The Condition of Labor," in *Five Great Encyclicals*. New York, Paulist Press, 1939.

Levinthal, Louis E. "Is Jewish Social Service Jewish?" *Jewish Education*, VIII, No. 1 (April–June, 1936), 63–66.

Levy, Charles S. "Attitudes towards Social Welfare: A Social Work Hurdle," *Journal of Jewish Communal Service*, XXXV, No. 4 (Summer, 1959), 393–400.

Lowell, C. Stanley. "New Day in Church and State," *World Outlook*, April, 1958.

—— *Separation and Religion*. Washington, D.C., Protestants and Other Americans United for Separation of Church and State, 1957.

McCluskey, Neil M., s.j. *Catholic Viewpoint on Education*. New York, Doubleday (Hanover House book), 1959.

Mannheim, Karl. *Diagnosis of Our Time*. London, Kegan Paul, 1943.

—— *Essays on the Sociology of Culture*. New York, Oxford University Press, 1956.

—— *Freedom, Power and Democratic Planning*. New York, Oxford University Press, 1950.

—— *Man and Society in an Age of Reconstruction*. New York, Harcourt, Brace, 1951.

—— *Systematic Sociology*. New York, Philosophical Library, 1957.

Maritain, Jacques. *Man and the State*. Chicago, University of Chicago Press, 1951.

Mayo, Leonard W. "Private vs. Public! Who's to Pay for Social Work?" *The Survey*, February, 1950.

Mayo, Leonard W. "Relationships between Public and Voluntary Health and Welfare Agencies, *Child Welfare*, XXXIX, No. 1 (January, 1960), 1–5.

――― "The Changing Role of Voluntary Agencies," *Social Work Journal*, XXXVI, No. 3 (July, 1955), 95–103.

Mead, Sidney E. "American Protestantism since the Civil War. II. From Americanism to Christianity," *Journal of Religion*, XXXVI, No. 2 (April, 1956), 67–89.

Mess, Henry A. *Voluntary Social Services since 1918*. London, Kegan Paul, 1948.

Michels, Robert. *Political Parties*. New York, Dover, 1959.

Miles, Arthur P. *An Introduction to Public Welfare*. Boston, Heath, 1949.

Miller, William Lee, et al. *Religion and the Free Society*. New York, Fund for the Republic, 1958.

Mills, C. Wright. *The Power Elite*. New York, Oxford University Press, 1956. (Paperback edition, Galaxy Books, 1959.)

Morris, Robert. "An Approach to a Rationale for Jewish Social Service," *Jewish Social Service Quarterly*, XXX, No. 1 (Fall, 1953), 51–62.

―――, and Arnold Gurin. "Community Relations Implications in the Use of Public Funds by Sectarian Agencies," *Journal of Jewish Communal Service*, XXXIII, No. 1 (Fall, 1956), 48–54.

Mosca, Gaetano. *The Ruling Class*. New York, McGraw-Hill, 1939.

Mueller, William A. *Church and State in Luther and Calvin: A Comparative Study*. Nashville, Broadman Press, 1954.

Murray, John Courtney. "Roman Catholic Church," *Annals of the American Academy of Political and Social Science*, CCLVI (March, 1948), 36–42.

National Social Welfare Assembly. *The Role of Voluntary Agencies in a Situation of Unemployment*. The Assembly, 1958.

New York City Department of Welfare, Bureau of Child Welfare. *Regulations and Instructions Governing the Administration of Reimbursement by City of New York to Voluntary Foster Care Agencies and Institutions*. The Bureau, 1960.

Niebuhr, H. Reinhold. *The Contribution of Religion to Social Work*. New York, Columbia University Press, 1932.

Niebuhr, H. Richard. *The Social Sources of Denominationalism*. New York, Meridian Books, 1957.

Nisbet, Robert. *The Quest for Community*. New York, Oxford University Press, 1953.

Nottingham, Elizabeth K. *Religion and Society*. New York, Doubleday, 1954.

Odegard, Peter H. "Toward a Responsible Bureaucracy," *Annals of the American Academy of Political and Social Science*, CCXCII (March, 1954), 18–29.

Our Bishops Speak: National Pastorals and Annual Statements of the Hierarchy of the United States (a compilation of pronouncements by the American Bishops and by committees of the National Catholic Welfare Conference from 1919 to 1951). Milwaukee, Bruce, 1952.

Parsons, Talcott. *Structure and Process in Modern Societies.* New York, Free Press, 1960.

Perlman, Max S. "Effect of Increased Public Funds on Jewish Federations and Agencies," *Journal of Jewish Communal Service*, XXXIV, No. 1 (Fall, 1957), 15–22.

Peyser, Dora. *The Strong and the Weak.* Sidney, Currawong, 1951.

Pfautz, Harold W. "The Sociology of Secularization," *American Journal of Sociology*, LXI, No. 2 (1955), 121–28.

Pfeffer, Leo. "Changing Relationships among Religious Groups," *Journal of Intergroup Relations*, I, No. 2 (Spring, 1960), 81–93.

Phenix, Philip H. "Religion in American Public Education," *Teachers College Record*, LVII, No. 1 (October, 1955), 26–31.

Pius XI. "Reconstructing the Social Order," in *Five Great Encyclicals.* New York, Paulist Press, 1939.

Pius XII. *Christmas Message, 1944, on Democracy.* New York, Paulist Press, 1955.

——— "Christmas Eve Address, 1952," *Catholic Mind*, February, 1953.

Polier, Justine Wise. "State, Religion and Child Welfare," *Journal of Jewish Communal Service*, XXXIII, No. 1 (Fall, 1956), 41–47.

Pound, Roscoe. "Religion and Social Control," *Rice Institute Pamphlet*, XXVII, No. 2 (April, 1940), 151–72.

Prinz, Joachim. "Ideology and Program," *Congress Weekly*, June 16, 1958, pp. 3–5.

Protestants and Other Americans United for Separation of Church and State. Sectarian Medical Codes and Your Tax Dollars. Washington, D.C., POAU, n.d.

Rabinoff, George W. "Jewish Communal Services and the American Scene," *Journal of Jewish Communal Service*, XXXVI, No. 1 (Fall, 1959), 4–13.

Randall, John Herman, Jr. "The Churches and the Liberal Tradition," *Annals of the American Academy of Political and Social Science*, CCLVI (March, 1948), 148–64.

Rheinstein, Max, ed. *Max Weber on Law in Economy and Society.* Cambridge, Mass., Harvard University Press, 1954.

Richmond, Mary E. *The Long View.* New York, Russell Sage Foundation, 1930.

Rooff, Madeline. *Voluntary Societies and Social Policy.* London, Routledge and Kegan Paul, 1957.

Ryan, William F. "C.S.G. and the Welfare State," *Social Order*, V, No. 6 (June, 1955), 270.

Schmidt, William D. "The Point of View of the Private Agency," *Child Welfare*, February, 1952 (special issue), pp. 15–16.

Sedren, A. L. "A Comment," *Journal of Jewish Communal Service*, XXXIV, No. 1 (Fall, 1957), 23–25.

Selig, Martha K. "Implications of the Use of Public Funds in Jewish Communal Services," *Journal of Jewish Communal Service*, XXXVI, No. 1 (Fall, 1959), 48–58.

Shulman, Charles E. "Charity in Three Languages," *Congress Weekly*, September 16, 1957, 9–11.

Siegfried, André. *America at Mid-Century*. New York, Harcourt, Brace, 1955.

––– *America Comes of Age*. New York, Harcourt, Brace, 1927.

Solander, Sanford. "Implications of Current National Trends for Jewish Health and Welfare Services," *Jewish Social Service Quarterly*, XXX, No. 1 (Fall, 1953), 26–32.

Spurlock, Clark. *Education and the Supreme Court*. Urbana, University of Illinois Press, 1955.

"State Control of Voluntary Social Work," editorial in *Catholic Charities Review*, XXXIV, No. 8 (October, 1950).

Stidley, Leonard Albert. *Sectarian Welfare Federation among Protestants*. New York, Association Press, 1944.

Sweet, William W. "The Protestant Churches," *Annals of American Academy of Political and Social Science*, CCLVI (March, 1948), 43–52.

Taylor, Maurice. "The Impact of the Changing Federal Welfare Program on Jewish Communal Activities," *Jewish Social Service Quarterly*, XXXI, No. 1 (Fall, 1954), 37–46.

Tocqueville, Alexis de. *Democracy in America*. Translated by Henry Reeve, Francis Bowen, and Phillip Bradley. New York, Alfred A. Knopf, 1925. 2 vols. (Reprinted, Vintage Books, 1957.)

Troeltsch, Ernst. *Protestantism and Progress*. Boston, Beacon Press, 1958.

Underwood, Kenneth Wilson. *Protestant and Catholic: Religious and Social Interaction in an Industrial Community*. Boston, Beacon Press, 1957.

Waldman, Saul. "Coverage of Ministers under Old-Age, Survivors, and Disability Insurance," *Social Security Bulletin*, XXIV, No. 4 (April, 1961), Social Security Administration, U.S. Department of Health, Education and Welfare, 18–21.

Weinstein, Jacob J. "The Responsibility of Jewish Community Services for the Preservation of Jewish Values: A Fixed Point of Reference," *Jewish Journal of Communal Service*, XXXV, No. 1 (Fall, 1958), 33–37.

Werner, Ruth M. *Public Financing of Voluntary Agency Foster Care*. New York, Child Welfare League of America, 1961.

Wickenden, Elizabeth. "Social Security and Voluntary Social Welfare," *Industrial and Labor Relations Review*, XIV, No. 1 (October, 1960), 94–106.

Wilensky, Harold L., and Charles N. Lebeaux. *Industrial Society and Social Welfare*. New York, Russell Sage Foundation, 1958.

Wright, Bishop John J. "Secularism in America," *Catholic Mind*, LVIII, No. 1152 (November–December, 1960), 493–97.

Yinger, J. Milton. *Religion in the Struggle for Power*. Durham, N.C., Duke University Press, 1946.

——— *Religion, Society and the Individual*. New York, Macmillan, 1957.

OTHER SOURCES

American Lutheran Church. "Broad Policies Governing the Relationships of the American Lutheran Church to Its Recognized Charitable Institutions and Welfare Agencies" (adopted by the Twelfth Convention of the American Lutheran Church, Waverley, Iowa, October 9–16, 1952). *Official Minutes*, pp. 465–68.

———, Board for Christian Social Action. "The Christian and His Public School" (statement of principles adopted by the American Lutheran Church at its Fifteenth Biennial Convention, San Antonio, Texas, October 9–16, 1958).

Baptist Joint Committee on Public Affairs. *Review and Evaluation of the C. E. Bryant Research into Allotment of Federal Funds to Churches*. Washington, D.C., the Committee, n.d.

Bernes, Martha C. Preliminary memorandum to the Federation of Jewish Philanthropy of New York on Federal Governmental Aid for Health and Welfare Programs, December 14, 1958. Mimeographed.

Bondy, Robert E. "Relationship between Public and Private Agency Programs" (address to the 26th Annual Session, Western Conference, Community Chests and Councils, Boys Hot Springs, Calif., April 3–6, 1950). In *Session Proceedings*. Mimeographed.

——— "The Interdependence of the Church and Social Welfare" (address to meeting of the Christian Social Welfare Associates, San Francisco, May 31, 1955). Mimeographed.

——— "The State of Voluntarism in Social Welfare Today" (statement at Conference of Executives, National Social Welfare Assembly, New York, June 15, 1960). Mimeographed.

Boyd, Beverley M. "A General Statement of Protestant Social Work and Its Relationship to Non-Church-related Agencies in the Total Community Pattern of Social Work" (paper presented at the Great Lakes Institute, College Camp, Wis., July 26–30, 1948). New York, Community Chests and Councils of America, mimeographed.

Brogan, Msgr. Bernard M., Director of Catholic Charities, Archdiocese of Chicago. Letter to the author, February 28, 1961.

Brown, James. "The Future of Private Child Caring Agencies" (address to the annual meeting of the Alton–Wood River Board of the Illinois Children's Home and Aid Society, March 10, 1949). Mimeographed.

Bryant, C. E. *Federal Aid to Religion as Shown in 1952*. (Research study made in behalf of the Baptist Joint Committee on Public Affairs, Washington, D.C., n.d.) Mimeographed.

Bureau of Social Research, Federation of Social Agencies of Pittsburgh and Allegheny County. *State Appropriations to Voluntary Welfare Organizations in Pennsylvania, 1931–1947* (results of a study made by the Bureau, dated March, 1948).

Catholic Charities. "The Care of Dependent, Neglected and Orphan Children—A Challenge to Our Faith" (statement of directors of Catholic Charities at their annual meeting, Atlantic City, N.J., November 17–18, 1949). Mimeographed.

Catholic Charities, Inc., of Portland, Oregon. *The Use of Public Funds by Private Agencies* (report based on replies to a questionnaire by 64 diocesan agencies of Catholic Charities). Portland, 1960, mimeographed.

Children's Bureau. *Report of the Advisory Council on Child Welfare Services*. Washington, D.C., U.S. Department of Health, Education and Welfare, Social Security Administration, December 28, 1959, mimeographed.

Child Welfare League of America, Inc. "A Statement of Principles and Policies on Public Child Welfare," February 20, 1950, mimeographed.

———— "A Statement of Principles and Policies on Private-Public Child Welfare Administration," July, 1958.

Churney, Paul R. "Division of Responsibility between Public and Private Agencies" (address to delegate meeting of the Child Welfare Division, Detroit Council on Social Agencies, March 15, 1949). Mimeographed.

Coady, Msgr. Leo J., Director of Catholic Charities, Archdiocese of Washington, D.C. Letter to the author, February 24, 1961.

Cogley, John. Summary statement at the Delaware Valley Seminar on Religion and the Free Society, sponsored by the National Conference of Christians and Jews, Philadelphia, May 19, 1959.

Community Chests and Councils of America. *Social Services under Catholic, Jewish, and Protestant Auspices in the Total Welfare System* (report of the Great Lakes Institute, Family and Children Services, Sec. 2, College Camp, Wis., July 26–30, 1948). New York, mimeographed.

———— and the American Social Welfare Assembly. *Determining Public-Voluntary Responsibility in the Light of Emerging Trends* (report of the Great Lakes Institute, College Camp, Wis., July 25–29, 1949). New York, mimeographed.

Cooke, Msgr. Vincent W., Archdiocesan Supervisor of Charities, Archdiocese of Chicago. Letter of April 1, 1949, to all directors of Catholic Charities in the United States. Mimeographed.

––– Memorandum to Msgr. John O'Grady, Executive Director of the National Catholic Welfare Conference, regarding Congressional Bill H.R. 2892. Mimeographed.

––– Memorandum on the [1950] White House Conference to Diocesan Directors of Charities in the United States. Mimeographed.

––– "Catholic Objectives in the Care of Children and How to Interpret Them" (address to the 35th annual meeting of the National Conference of Catholic Charities, Atlantic City, N.J., November 20, 1949). MS made available by Msgr. Bernard Brogan, Catholic Charities, Chicago.

––– "The Infiltration of Secularism into the Catholic Social Field" (address to the National Congress for Religious of the United States, University of Notre Dame, Notre Dame, Ind., August 12, 1952). Mimeographed.

Council of Jewish Federations and Welfare Funds. "Public Welfare–Local Federation Responsibilities" (report of a workshop session held in Detroit, November 10–13, 1960). Mimeographed.

Dawson, John B. *Transfers from Chest to Public Financing* (report by the Executive Director of the Health and Welfare Council of Philadelphia, April 20, 1953). Mimeographed.

Delaware County District Health and Welfare Council. *Recommendations on Function and Responsibility of Public and Private City Chest Supported Child Care Agencies in Delaware County, Philadelphia* (report of the Children's Committee of the Council, June 25, 1951). Mimeographed.

Dumpson, James R. "Public and Private Agency Responsibility" (address to the Connecticut State Conference of Social Welfare, Hartford, November 19, 1957). MS.

Eustace, Bartholomew J., Bishop of Camden. "Charity, Industry and the Welfare State" (address to the 35th annual National Conference of Catholic Charities, Atlantic City, N.J., November 20, 1949). MS made available by Msgr. Bernard Brogan, Catholic Charities, Chicago.

Ewing, Oscar R. "The Partnership of Government and Voluntary Welfare Agencies" (address to the General Assembly, Council of Jewish Federations and Welfare Funds, Washington, D.C., December 2, 1950). Mimeographed.

Fink, Joseph L. "Summary of C.C.A.R. Opinion on Church and State as Embodied in Resolutions Adopted at Conferences through the Years" (report of the Chairman of the Church and State Committee of the Central Conference of American Rabbis). Philadelphia, Jewish Publication Society, 1948.

Flanagan, Msgr. William J. "The Future of Catholic Charities and Child Care" (address to the 35th annual National Conference of Catholic Charities, Atlantic City, N.J., November 20, 1949). Mimeographed. Made available by Msgr. Bernard Brogan, Catholic Charities, Chicago.

Flynn, Rev. James B., Diocesan Executive Director of Social Service, Archdiocese of San Francisco. Letter to the author, June 2, 1961.

Gallagher, Msgr. Raymond J., Assistant Director of Catholic Charities Bureau, Cleveland Diocese. Letter to the author, February 13, 1961.

——— Statement at a meeting of Protestant and Catholic welfare leaders, New York, April 9, 1958. Mimeographed.

——— "The Place of Government in Welfare" (statement at the Second National Conference on the Churches and Social Welfare, National Council of the Churches of Christ in the U.S.A., Cleveland, October 25, 1961). MS.

General Assembly of the Presbyterian Church, U.S.A., *Christian Social Action* (social pronouncements of the 161st General Assembly, adopted May 25, 1949). Philadelphia, Board of Christian Education, Presbyterian Church, U.S.A., Division of Social Education and Action, 1949.

Guilfoyle, Bishop George H. Statement before the Subcommittee on Public Welfare of the Temporary State Commission on Coordination of State Activities of the State of New York, n.d. Mimeographed.

——— "The Role of Public Welfare" (paper presented to a group of Protestant leaders at the National Council of the Churches of Christ in the U.S.A., December, 1960). Mimeographed.

Haas, Harold, Executive Secretary of the Board of Social Missions of the United Lutheran Church of America. Letter to the author, February 13, 1961.

Health and Welfare Council of Metropolitan St. Louis. "Position Statement on Governmental and Voluntary Agencies Providing Leisure Time Services: Their Functions and Relationships" (statement by the Group Work and Recreation Division of the Council, April, 1955). Mimeographed.

Health and Welfare Council of National Capital Area. *Payments by Public Agencies for Voluntary Health and Welfare Services* (staff report prepared by Thomas W. Fetzer, Assistant Executive Director of the Council, September, 1959). Mimeographed.

Health and Welfare Council of Philadelphia. *Manual on the Financing of Child Care Services in Philadelphia* (prepared by the Committee on Public and Private Financing of the Council, July 23, 1953). Mimeographed.

——— *Public and Private Financing* (report of the Subcommittee on Financing of Child Care Services, December 23, 1953). Mimeographed.

——— *Report of the Subcommittee on General Principles Regarding Di-*

vision of Responsibility between Public and Private Financing of Health and Welfare Services (December 17, 1953). Mimeographed.

——— "Voluntary and Tax Support for Health and Welfare Services" (statement, May 8, 1953). Mimeographed.

Hexter, Maurice B. "Voluntarism in Sectarian Social Work" (paper presented at symposium on Voluntarism in Social Welfare, Brandeis University, Waltham, Mass., June 10, 1961).

Johnson, Arlien. "Use of Public Funds by Voluntary Agencies" (address to the National Conference of Social Welfare, Section 3, San Francisco, May 25, 1959). Mimeographed.

Johnson, F. Ernest. Summary of statement made at the Delaware Valley Seminar on Religion and the Free Society, The Nature of Religious Pluralism (dialogue program sponsored by the National Conference of Christians and Jews, Philadelphia, May 19, 1959).

Johnson, Msgr. William R., Director of Catholic Charities, Archdiocese of Los Angeles. Letter to the author, March 21, 1961.

Kahn, Dorothy C. "Public-Private Responsibility in Joint Planning" (paper presented at New York State Conference on Social Work, Albany, November 14, 1947). Mimeographed.

Kramer, Ralph M. "The Changing Role of County Welfare Departments in the Community" (paper presented at the Public Assistance Section of the 46th Annual State Conference on Health, Welfare and Recreation, San Jose, Calif., n.d.). Mimeographed.

Krumbholz, C. E. "Social Welfare and the Protestant Denominations" (address to the joint session of the Division of Christian Life and Work and the Division of Home Missions of the National Council of the Churches of Christ in the U.S.A., Buck Hill Falls, Pa., December 12, 1951).

Lawler, Msgr. Daniel E., Director of Diocesan Charities and Welfare, Diocese of Syracuse. Letter to the author, February 20, 1961.

Lee, John Park, Executive Secretary of the National Presbyterian Health and Welfare Association. "The State of Voluntarism in Social Welfare Today" (statement at conference of executives sponsored by the National Social Welfare Assembly, New York, September 28, 1960). Mimeographed.

——— "Why We Are Here" (address to the opening of the First Biennial Conference of the National Presbyterian Health and Welfare Association, Chicago, February 27, 1957). Mimeographed.

Lenroot, Katherine. "Child Welfare—A Challenge to Both Private and Public Agencies" (address to the 67th annual meeting of the Illinois Children's Home and Aid Society, January 5, 1950). [Reprinted in Home Life for Children, Vol. XXXVII, No. 1 (Spring, 1950).]

Lurie, Harry L. "Approach and Philosophy of Jewish Social Welfare" (address to the Great Lakes Institute, College Camp, Wis., July 26–30, 1948). New York, Community Chests and Councils of America, mimeographed.

Manser, George. "Public-Private Responsibility in the Casework Field" (paper presented at the Biennial Conference, United Community Funds and Councils, Detroit, February 8, 1956). Mimeographed.

Mayo, Leonard, President of the Child Welfare League of America. Open letter of April 15, 1950, to the state governors of the United States.

Mayor's Committee of Inquiry on New York City Department of Welfare. Report submitted September 30, 1959, Maurice B. Hexter, Chairman. Mimeographed.

Methodist Church, Board of Social and Economic Relations. *Research Consultation on the Church and State* (reports of the Third Assembly, New York East Conference, Tuxedo Park, N.Y., September 8–10, 1959). Chicago, 1960, mimeographed.

––– *Research Consultation on the Church and State* (reports of the Fourth Assembly, New York East Conference, Tuxedo Park, N.Y., January 21–23, 1960). Mimeographed.

Millar, Walter P., Jr. Statement to Board of Directors of the Health and Welfare Council, Philadelphia, January 4, 1954.

Miller, Haskell M. "Government's Role in Social Welfare" (statement at the Second National Conference on the Churches and Social Welfare, National Council of the Churches of Christ in the U.S.A., Cleveland, October 23–27, 1961). Mimeographed.

National Catholic Welfare Conference. "Need for Personal Responsibility" (statement of the Bishops of the United States, signed by the members of the Administrative Board, National Catholic Welfare Conference, in the name of the Bishops, October, 1960).

National Conference of Christians and Jews. *The Nature of Religious Pluralism* (dialogue program at the Delaware Valley Seminar on Religion and the Free Society sponsored by the Conference, Philadelphia, May 19, 1959).

National Council of the Churches of Christ in the U.S.A. *Policy and Strategy in Social Welfare: Report to the Churches.* New York, Department of Social Welfare, Division of Christian Life and Work, National Council of Churches, 1957.

National Lutheran Council. "A Christian Affirmation for Lutheran Health and Welfare" (from the Executive Committee, Division of Welfare, National Lutheran Council, *Minutes*, Appendix A, December 10, 1958).

––– *Christ Frees and Unites . . . for Responsible Service* (reports of the Lutheran World Conference on Social Responsibility, Wittenberg

College, Springfield, Ohio, August 7–10, 1957). New York, Division of Welfare, National Lutheran Council.

National Presbyterian Health and Welfare Association. "Our Church and People's Needs" (statement of Presbyterian Church and Welfare approved by the 169th General Assembly, Omaha, 1957).

——— "Presbyterian Church and Welfare" (statement by the 169th General Assembly of the Presbyterian Church in the U.S.A., Omaha, May 21, 1957). Mimeographed.

——— "Report of Special Hospital Study Committee of the National Presbyterian Health and Welfare Association" (approved by the Board of National Missions and adopted by the 171st General Assembly, Indianapolis, May 26, 1959).

National Social Welfare Assembly. *Changing Role of Government in Social Welfare* (report of spring meeting, New York, April, 1957). Mimeographed.

——— *Committee on Social Issues and Policies–Report of Subcommittee on Tax Exemption.* December 16, 1957. Mimeographed.

Nygren, Anders. "The Contexts within Which the Church Develops Responsible Service" (address to the Lutheran World Conference on Social Responsibility, Wittenberg College, Springfield, Ohio, August 8, 1957). New York, Division of Welfare, National Lutheran Council, 1957.

Oakland [Calif.] Council of Churches, Community Welfare Council. *Final Report of the Committee on Social Welfare Programs* (March, 1954). Mimeographed.

O'Donnell, Tom, Director of Catholic Family Service, Catholic Charities of Saint Louis. Letter to the author, March 27, 1961.

O'Grady, Msgr. John, Executive Director of the National Catholic Welfare Conference. Letter of March 21, 1950, to the State Department of Social Welfare, Lansing, Mich.

——— "Church Responsibility for Social Welfare" (address to the Great Lakes Institute, College Camp, Wis., July 26–30, 1948). New York, Community Chests and Councils of America, mimeographed.

——— Statement before the Ways and Means Committee of the U.S. House of Representatives concerning H.R. 2892, Public Welfare Act of 1949, on March 10, 1949.

——— "Implications of the Proposed Public Assistance Program" (address to the New England Regional Conference of Catholic Charities, Providence, March 28, 1949). Mimeographed.

Ohio Department of Public Welfare. *Recommendations of the Ohio State Child Welfare Advisory Committee Regarding the Division of Responsibility between Public and Private Children's Agencies.* Department of Public Welfare, Division of Social Administration, Children's Services, May 1, 1946. MS.

President of the Advisory Board of the Hartford Diocesan Bureau of
Social Service. Letter of October 21, 1960, to Bernard Shapiro, Commissioner of the Connecticut State Welfare Department.

Protestant Conference on Child Welfare. *The Nation's Children, the
Churches' Responsibility* (report of Conference held at Columbus,
Ohio, October 18–19, 1949). Chicago, International Council of Reli-
gious Education, 1950.

"Public and Private Agencies' Responsibilities in the Field of Social Wel-
fare" (working notes for the Commissioner by the Bureau of Public
Assistance, Social Security Administration, Federal Security Agency,
December 1, 1949). MS.

Reese, Rev. Thomas J., Director of the Catholic Welfare Guild, Diocese
of Wilmington, Delaware. Letter to the author, April 3, 1961.

Reid, Joseph H., Executive Director of the Child Welfare League of
America. Letter to the author, February 16, 1961.

Résumé—Meeting of Roman Catholic and Protestant Welfare Leaders
(New York, September 17, 1958, Arlette R. Pederson, recorder).
Mimeographed.

Rilley, Msgr. Thomas J., Director of Catholic Charities, Archdiocese of
Philadelphia. Letter to the author, February 17, 1961.

Rockwell, Rev. Lee W., Executive Secretary of the Commission on
Health and Welfare Services, Evangelical and Reformed Church
(United Church of Christ), Philadelphia. Letter to the author, March
17, 1961.

Ropchcan, Alexander. "The Division of Responsibility between Governmental and Voluntary Agencies—Health Field" (address delivered to
the Midwest Conference, Community Chests and Councils of America,
Chicago, February 11, 1955).

Saveth, Edward N. "Religion and the Welfare State." New York, American Jewish Committee, 1952. MS.

Schottland, Charles I. "Use of Public Funds by Jewish Agencies" (paper
presented at the 27th General Assembly of the Council of Jewish
Federations and Welfare Funds, Washington, D.C., November 13–16,
1958). Mimeographed.

——— "The Relationship of Public and Private Agencies" (lecture before
Seminar in Modern American Philanthropy, Brandeis University,
Waltham, Mass., February, 1961). Notes in the files of the author.

Selig, Martha K. "Income from Public Sources" (paper presented at the
27th General Assembly of the Council of Jewish Federations and Welfare Funds, Washington, D.C., November 13–16, 1958).

Sise, Rev. John R., Diocesan Director of Catholic Charities, Diocese of
Albany. Letter to the author, February 17, 1961.

Suedkamp, Msgr. W., Secretary for Charities, Archdiocese of Detroit.
Letter to the author, March 14, 1961.

Synagogue Council of America and the National Community Relations Advisory Council. "Safeguarding Religious Liberty" (a joint statement). New York, Joint Advisory Committee of S.C.A. and N.C.R.A.C., 1957.

United Community Funds and Councils of America and the American Social Welfare Assembly. *A New Look at Governmental and Voluntary Services* (proceedings of the Adirondack Workshop, Silver Bay, N.Y., August 10–14, 1953). New York, mimeographed.

United Community Services, Committee on Relationship of Tax-Supported and Voluntary Health and Welfare Agencies by Fields of Service. *Policies on United Community Services of Metropolitan Boston* (report of the Committee adopted by the Board of United Community Services, January 27, 1955).

United Nations Economic and Social Council. *The Development of National Social Service Programmes* (report by a group of experts appointed by the Secretary-General of the Social Commission, Twelfth Session, E/Cn.5/333, March 9, 1959). Mimeographed.

——— *Scope and Development of National Social Service Programs* (report by the Secretary-General of the Social Commission, Twelfth Session, E/Cn.5/333/Add.1, March 30, 1959). Mimeographed.

Villaume, Rev. William J. "Under What Conditions and with What Objectives Should Voluntary Agencies, Including Church-Related Agencies, Accept Public Funds?" (paper presented at a meeting of Roman Catholic and Protestant welfare leaders, New York, September 17, 1958). Mimeographed.

——— "Church-State Relations in Social Welfare—An Introduction" (paper presented to a group of clergymen concerned with church-state relations in America, New York, November, 1958). Mimeographed.

——— "Church-State Relations in Social Welfare" (abstract of a paper presented at the New York East Conference of the Methodist Church, Board of Social and Economic Relations, Third Assembly, Tuxedo Park, N.Y., September 8–10, 1959). Mimeographed.

Wedel, Mrs. Theodore O. "Health and Welfare Needs of the Nation and the Place of the Church Agency" (address at a dinner attended by the Episcopal Eishop of New York and members of the Department of Christian Social Relations of the Diocese of New York, New York, January 12, 1954). New York, Department of Christian Social Relations of the Episcopal Church.

Weil, Frank L. "Cooperation of the Church in Social Work" (address delivered at the 76th Annual Meeting of the National Conference of Social Welfare, Cleveland, June 17, 1949). National Social Welfare Assembly.

Welfare Council of Metropolitan Chicago. *Report of the Welfare Council of Metropolitan Chicago to the Community Fund on Principles and*

Their Application of Division Responsibility between Voluntary and Tax-Supported Welfare Services (approved by the Board of Directors, April 16, 1947, and reaffirmed by the Board of Directors of the Council, November 16, 1955). Mimeographed.

Welfare Federation of Cleveland. "Guiding Principles on Division of Work between the Publically Administered and Privately Administered Health and Welfare Organizations" (statement of principles by the Federation, June, 1955). Mimeographed.

Welfare Planning Council, Los Angeles Region. *Report: Public-Private Responsibility for Recreation, Group-Work and Informal Education* (report of the Youth Services Division of the Council, May 11, 1956). Mimeographed.

Wickenden, Elizabeth. "The State of Voluntarism in Social Welfare Today" (statement at Conference of Executives, sponsored by the National Social Welfare Assembly, New York, September 28, 1960). Mimeographed.

Willen, Joseph. "The Responsibility of Jewish Agencies to Today's American Community" (address to the 28th General Assembly, Council of Jewish Federations and Welfare Funds, San Francisco, November 13, 1959). Mimeographed.

Williams, J. Peter, President of the Health and Welfare Council, Philadelphia. "Suggested Communication to Community Chest of Philadelphia and Vicinity on Public and Private Financing" (open letter, January 18, 1954, to Elias Wolf, President of the Community Chest of Philadelphia). Mimeographed.

Willman, Clara, Supervisor, Child Service Unit, Department of Public Assistance, State of Washington. Personal letter, June 28, 1961.

Witte, Edgar F. "The Philosophy and Program of Lutheran Welfare" (address to the Great Lakes Institute, College Camp, Wis., July 26–30, 1948). New York, Community Chests and Councils of America, mimeographed.

INDEX